THE FIRST TRANSATLANTIC FLIGHT, 1919

HY STEIRMAN
& GLENN D. KITTLER

CW00828731

A DRUM BOOK
1986

TO EVELYN SINGER HABER,OUR AGENT...
...BECAUSE SHE BELIEVED

THE FIRST TRANSATLANTIC FLIGHT, 1919

All Rights Reserved
Copyright © 1961, 1986, by Hy Steirman and Glenn D. Kittler

ISBN 0-931933-19-6

Library of Congress catalog number: 81-10216

Originally published by Harper & Row under the title TRIUMPH.

Richardson & Steirman
246 Fifth Avenue
New York, NY 10001

PRINTED IN CANADA

Acknowledgments

WRITING THIS BOOK about the first transatlantic flight has proved to be almost as great an adventure as the flight itself. For five years we have engaged in fascinating detective work, hunting out the men who made the flight and correlating their dramatic experiences with the official records. Shakespeare once observed that "old men remember with advantages." In this case, the advantages were important in terms of accuracy. We were overjoyed when we discovered that, for forty years, the men we interviewed had kept both their files and their memories uncluttered. Undoubtedly, this is a tribute to their Navy training. When our research was finished, we found we were able to put together the widely scattered pieces of this vital moment of aviation history with astonishing accuracy and fidelity. Men who had not seen each other in years recalled conversations practically verbatim; personal records gave special life to crisp official documents; the tensions, heartaches and dangers of the flight became real when related by the men who had suffered them. Thus we have been able, we feel, to re-create the triumph of NCs in both the technical and personal detail that is rarely available to those who write about heroic hours such as these.

We are particularly indebted to Rear Admiral and Mrs. Albert C. Read for their time and hospitality on several visits to their home in Washington, D.C., Virginia Beach and Miami. The long hours we talked and examined scrapbooks and documents, including the Admiral's log of the flight, were important encouragement throughout the years of research. Equally encouraging was the eight-hour interview during which James L. Breese allowed us to tape his intimate memories of the flight at his California home. The comedian of the flight, Mr. Breese was seriously ill when we met him but he insisted on continuing the interview despite the rest periods that were repeatedly necessary for him. His wit and charm stirred our deep affection for him; his pride in being part of the flight won our admiration. When he died soon after our meeting we felt a personal loss. We deeply felt the loss, too, of Captain H. C. Richardson, designer of the NC hulls, who while puffing on the enormous cigars he enjoyed gave us important technical information of the flight at our meetings in Washington. Here was another man justly proud of the flight, for not only was Captain Richardson important in making the experience possible but he also underwent the worst moments of it on the high seas and he lived to see the vital contributions his own genius made to Naval aviation.

Also in Washington we received important help from Vice Admiral Pat Bellinger and Captain R. A. Lavender. In New York, Lt. Harry Sadenwater clarified details regarding radio communications on the planes; and on a rainy St. Patrick's Day, Mrs. John H. Towers, widow of the man who actually arranged the flight and commanded it, welcomed us into her Manhattan house to share her memories of this great Navy hero. The regular letters from Eugene S. Rhoads, of Los Angeles, provided us with the encouragement we needed during the months of writing his experiences as the lone enlisted man aboard the triumphant plane. William Shigley, of Maywood, California, who was a member of the ground crew, supplied important details of the pre-flight problems and successes. General Lester Maitland, who incidentally was the first man to fly the Pacific to Hawaii, gave us the benefit of his personal acquaintance with the Navy pilots during our visit with him at Red Bluff, California, where he is now an Episcopal priest.

To the United States Navy goes our deep bow of gratitude for immeasurable assistance at every point of our work. Men like Captain Wade De Weese, Commander Russell L. Bufkins, Lt. Commanders H. G. Gimpel and F. A. Prehn, and Adrian O. Van Wyen and Greg J. Kennedy helped greatly in the Pentagon, the Navy Historical Section, the Navy Photographic Center, the Navy Film Depository, the National Archives and the U.S. Naval Academy. Without the aid of these men we would not have been able to substantiate, with pictures and documents, the various reports we obtained from newspapers and magazines.

As for the press, we are grateful for use of eye-witness

reports that appeared in the *New York Times,* the old New York *World,* the Washington *Post,* the London *Times,* the London *Illustrated News* and the London *Graphic.* The Lord Mayor F. S. Scott of Plymouth, England, was helpful in providing records from his city's archives. Herman Kahn, director of the Franklin D. Roosevelt Library, Hyde Park, New York, contributed data regarding President Roosevelt's active interest in the flight. We also received assistance from the research staffs of the New York Public Library, the White Plains, New York, Public Library and the Curtiss-Wright Corporation, Wood-Ridge, New Jersey.

Outstanding co-operation was granted us by Dr. Paul Garber, chief curator of the National Air Museum at the Smithsonian Institution. It was, in fact, Doctor Garber who was responsible for having the NC-4 reassembled and displayed at the museum thirty years after her flight. "The most overlooked aircraft in history," he called her. And when he learned of our interest in her and her sister ships, his personal interest in their flight and his eagerness for their recognition, now in the era of outer space, was our first and most lasting encouragement. Philip S. Hopkins, director of the museum, was equally enthusiastic.

At last, when the research was finished and the chore of writing began, we were happy recipients of the skillful advice of Evan Thomas and Miss Gene Young, of Harper & Brothers, and Mrs. Patricia Friel and Miss Alice Kenner, our patient editorial assistants.

To all these we extend our gratitude. We know they all share our hope that this belated tribute to the pioneers of fifty years of Naval aviation adequately salutes their courage and their triumphs.

HY STEIRMAN AND GLENN D. KITTLER

viii

I

THE MORNING was chilly and overcast. A brisk wind came out of the west and pushed a three-day storm back to sea. Newspaper reporters who had spent a week on the beach looked at the gray sky and wondered if at last this might be the day. At a press conference the night before, they had been told that most likely the take-off would be delayed thirty-six hours to give the storm time to dissipate itself at sea, and the morning papers carried this news. Because of it, the hundreds of New Yorkers who had flocked to Rockaway Beach in horseless carriages each day now remained at home. The beach was quiet and empty.

There were many people who had begun to doubt that the

flight would ever take place. The very idea of it was too bold, too daring, too outrageous. Aviation was only sixteen years old. Just eight years before, Glenn Curtiss had lifted the first seaplane into the air over San Diego Bay. Despite their effective use in the World War, planes, whether land or sea, were considered little more than toys or circus attractions. None that had succeeded in getting into the air weighed more than a thousand pounds. And now, on this dismal May morning of 1919, there sat on the beach of the Naval Air Station at Rockaway, New York, three monstrous seaplanes, each with a wingspan of 126 feet, a hull of over 45 feet, and weighing more than 22,000 pounds, and these, the Navy had announced, would be used to fly across the Atlantic Ocean. You might just as well put wings on the Woolworth Building and expect it to make the flight.

The Navy was determined to try.

Shortly after seven o'clock on the Thursday morning of May 8, weather reports began to arrive at the Rockaway station. From ships at sea and from Coast Guard lookouts along the Eastern seaboard came assurances that the gale which had kept the three huge planes landlocked for almost a week had moved out of the way. By eight o'clock, airmen had rolled two of the big planes out of their hangar to join the third that had spent the night on the beach. The hangar was the largest ever to be constructed, and originally it had been designed to accommodate four of the immense ships, but as the planes took shape it was found that only two could fit inside the hangar at one time. The short estimate had been another joke on the Navy: once again the highly organized military mind had proved that it didn't know what it was doing.

The reporters, down on the beach after early breakfasts, had witnessed these morning exercises before and were not impressed by them. For that matter, there was such widespread skepticism about the flight that as yet it had not made the front pages of any New York papers. For the reporters, the assignment was something of a death watch. In their opinion, the men who really had the exciting job were up at Newfoundland, where teams of British pilots were preparing for the race across the Atlantic for the fifty-thousand-dollar prize offered by the London *Daily Mail*. The Navy had declared that the scheduling of its own transatlantic efforts at the same time as the British contest had been coincidental, that the Navy pilots would not be permitted to accept the prize money even if they won it. For the Navy, the flight was an experiment. No risks would be taken with the lives of the crews or with the expensive equipment. By its calmness, sobriety, planning and patience, the Navy had stripped itself of drama.

At nine o'clock, a small truck arrived, and sailors began carrying parcels from it to the three planes. Curious, the New York *World* man drifted over, watched for a moment, then asked, "What have you got there?"

"Chow," said one of the sailors.

"For the crews?"

"I guess so."

"Are they taking off?"

"Looks like it."

The *World* man turned and headed back toward the other reporters. "Something's up," he said.

A yeoman stepped to them. "Commander Towers wants to talk to you men in the hangar office."

The reporters followed him back to the hangar. The Brooklyn *Times* man asked, "Is this it, Sonny?"

The yeoman frowned over his shoulder. "Wait and see, Dad."

The reporters entered a small crowded room. At the opposite end, they saw a cluster of men in one-piece flight suits gathered around Commander John H. Towers. A tall, lean man with a piercing scowl, Towers heard the reporters and turned to them. He waited a moment, then:

"This will be brief," he said. "We are taking off in an hour." He glanced at them, expecting a reaction, but there was none. He went on: "You've already been given a list of the crews and you know our route. The storm has passed far enough to sea for us to get started. If we don't have any more trouble, we could be at Halifax in approximately five hours."

There had already been trouble enough. Four of the planes had been built for the flight. In March, a sudden storm ripped one ship from its moorings and sent it crashing against a pier, damaging it beyond repair. Then, just a few days later, a fire broke out while the ships were being fueled, badly burning the wings of one and the tail of another. Both planes were repaired with parts cannibalized from the storm-damaged ship. To climax the streak of bad luck, on Friday, a skilled machinist, scheduled to go on the flight, had carelessly moved too close to a twirling propeller: his right hand was cut off neatly at the wrist. Too dazed to realize what had happened to him, the man made his way slowly to the first-aid station, calling back to his crew: "I'll be all right. Don't go without me. Just don't go without me."

Towers told the reporters, "I hope you haven't many questions because we haven't got much time."

The *New York Times* asked, "Any changes in plans since we talked to you last night?"

"No, none," said Towers.

There was silence. Then someone at the back said, "Good luck, Commander."

4

Towers said, "Thank you."

The meeting broke up. The crews went out to their planes.

News that the flight was about to start traveled through the air station. All work was stopped. A thousand Navy officers and enlisted men hiked across the sand to the beach in front of the hangar. The reporters, some civilians from nearby towns and a handful of Navy brass from Washington added two hundred more to the crowd.

At five minutes to ten, two of the planes were rolled onto railways and guided into the water, their engines coughing and sputtering uncertainly. At ten o'clock, the third ship was rolled into runway position. There was a moment's wait until the two advance ships moved out of the way, then the last plane slid down the rails and into the water. Now the waiting was over. Without pausing, the three planes taxied into the deeper waters of Jamaica Bay, turned westward into the wind and took off. Two miles away they gained an altitude of five hundred feet, then they made a complete turn and headed eastward, passing over the air station.

The crowd on the beach was strangely quiet. There had been no shouts as the planes took off, no cheers as they passed overhead. This was, as everyone acknowledged, an auspicious moment for the Navy: its first aircraft had now been commissioned as a distinct Fleet division and its first pilots were now embarked on a momentous flight. Yet no Navy vessel had ever been launched with less occasion, less hope, less pride, less ceremony. There had been merely this:

Earlier in the week, Captain M. A. Irwin, of the Aviation Section of the Naval Bureau of Operations, had arrived from Washington and he brought with him a small box of four-leaf clovers. He was beginning to wonder if the twigs would wither before the ships got off the water. Then, just before the crews climbed into their planes, he passed among the men, shaking their hands and giving them the clovers for good luck.

They would need it.

2

At first nobody knew what to call the big planes. During the early months of their design the engineers at the Glenn Curtiss Aeroplane & Motor Corporation at Buffalo had labeled their blueprints with "TH," for the sake of their own filing system. But "TH" meant nothing to the Navy. It occurred to Commander G. C. Westervelt, a Navy construction engineer, to call the planes DWTs, after Rear Admiral Douglas W. Taylor, chief of the Bureau of Construction, but word seeped through the ranks that the Admiral didn't think much of the idea. Westervelt then created a new name: NCs —derived from the fact that both the Navy and Curtiss were involved in the production. When the planes eventually came to public attention, reporters nicknamed them the Nancies, a name that implied both derision and affection.

Many men concerned with the NCs held the same mixed emotions toward them. Even on paper they looked like an engineer's impractical joke. They were to be the biggest heavier-than-air craft to be built in aviation's short history, and the first obstacle was that no engine existed with the power to lift them. Nevertheless, the dangers of war turned the joke into a challenge.

The dangers began even before the United States entered the war. In Europe, airplanes had proved their worth in the observation of enemy troop movements. Obviously, there had to be some defense against such observations, and the best defense was more planes, now armed to fight the observers off. Armed planes then became vital weapons, strafing troops and truck convoys. The progression to using planes as bombers was inevitable.

But planes were hard to come by. Most of the ships used in Europe were hand-made; at the start of the war, many of the planes were privately owned and were flown in combat by their owners. As the war spread, the need for more planes, a lot of planes, became quite clear. In all the world, there was only one company that had developed a system of assembly-line production of planes that could come anywhere near meeting the demand: Curtiss, on the banks of the Niagara River in Buffalo.

Glenn Hammond Curtiss worked his way into the airplane business by the devious route of bicycles, motorcycles and gliders. Early in life he developed a love of speed, but he was a mechanic more than a sportsman, more interested in making speed possible than in speeding himself. He was born in Hammondsport, on Long Island, in 1878, and his father's death forced him to go to work before he was ten. He was employed by the Eastman Kodak Company in Rochester, assembling cameras for four dollars a week. He was still in his teens when he returned to Hammondsport and, to earn money, opened a bicycle repair shop. Bicycle racing was a popular sport; Curtiss spent so much time redesigning bicycles for racing that his business failed.

He spent the next few years as an auto mechanic in the repair shops that were beginning to appear throughout the country. Cars didn't interest him as vehicles of speed. In his twenties, he took another stab at his bicycle business, this time concentrating more on motorcycles. By building his own motors, he found he could get more speed out of them. In 1904, he set a record of ten miles in eight minutes and fifty-four seconds—phenomenal speed for the time. A few years later he made a mile in twenty-six and two-fifths seconds—137 miles an hour, which was then faster than anything on earth.

Curtiss's interest in aviation was a natural evolution. Aviation meant speed. His first endeavor in the field came when Captain Thomas Baldwin, a famous dirigible pilot, traveled all the way from California to Hammondsport in 1904 to ask Curtiss to build a high-speed engine for his dirigible. That year, Baldwin astounded the crowds at the St. Louis World's Fair by whizzing over their heads at speeds up to ten miles an hour. Through Baldwin, Curtiss made his first contacts with the Army and Navy Departments. When the Army ordered its first dirigible, Curtiss built it. It achieved the alarming speed of twenty miles an hour.

By now Curtiss had become a celebrity. Dr. Alexander Graham Bell, the inventor of the telephone, invited him to Nova Scotia in 1905 to discuss organizing a society for the promotion of flying. Another member of Bell's group was Lieutenant Thomas Selfridge, of the U.S. Army. Three years later Selfridge became the first man to die in an air accident, when the plane in which he was flying with Orville Wright crashed at Fort Myer, Virginia.

Because of the construction facilities at Hammondsport, Bell's group decided to make its headquarters there. On money provided by Mrs. Bell, the group first devoted itself to gliders in order to learn the problems of controlling a plane once it got into the air. The youngest of the group and the most daring, Curtiss did most of the flying. The experience developed him into a skilled pilot, one of the best of his day. He was the first pilot to turn a plane while in flight, a particularly outstanding feat in view of the fact that everybody else was too concerned during their few moments of flight with keeping themselves and their planes in one piece. Curtiss's skill served him well during legal difficulties on

8

patent rights in 1914. Attorneys for the Wright brothers accused Curtiss of including Wright patents in his own designs without paying for them. Curtiss argued that if he were expanding on anybody's designs it was those of Samuel P. Langley. As early as 1896, Langley, working with power-driven models, proved that mechanical flight was possible. A famous scientist, Langley was secretary of the Smithsonian Institution, which put him in an effective position to win War Department financial support to build a plane in 1903. Just at the time the Wright brothers were working at Kitty Hawk, Langley made two attempts to fly his plane across the Potomac, but both times it merely tumbled down a hill and into the drink. In view of this, the Wright attorneys pointed out that Curtiss could hardly have used the Langley inventions because obviously they didn't work. Curtiss insisted: "They did work, and if Langley's plane didn't fly it was only because he was such a lousy pilot." As proof, Curtiss paid to have Langley's plane rebuilt, accurately and to the most intimate detail, then he took it out and flew it.

The first plane Curtiss built for the Bell group flew 318 feet and 11 inches before it crash-landed. The second plane flew 1,017 feet and Curtiss landed it safely. In the third plane he flew a kilometer and won the *Scientific American* trophy. On May 31, 1910, he won ten thousand dollars in prize money from the New York *World* by flying from Albany to New York, a 150-mile trip which he made with two stops en route to refuel. It was the greatest flight of the age.

3

Now having wings, man could not be held down. The continent became a runway for pilots, who needed only a pasture to take off or land in their slow-moving planes. The seas beckoned, and it seemed there would be no peace among pilots until someone managed to fly across them.

The first American attempt was made in a strange oblong contraption, 228 feet long. It was called the *America,* and it was made by Walter Wellman, a writer-adventurer, and Melvin Vaniman, a wealthy engineer. On October 15, 1910, they took off from Atlantic City for Europe. Two days later, after some helter-skelter flying, they were forced to dump their engines in an effort to keep the airship aloft. But it crashed, and after eighteen days at sea they were picked up by the steamer *Trent,* 375 miles east of Norfolk, Virginia. Despite their failure, they were heroes and were given a ticker-tape welcome to New York City. To their credit was an air coverage of a thousand miles, even though they had little control over where they went.

Melvin Vaniman remained determined to fly the Atlantic. By 1912 he had built another dirigible-type airship, this one 258 feet long and called the *Akron.* On July 1, with Vaniman, his brother and three friends aboard, the ship took off from Atlantic City and cruised at five hundred feet over the heads of an amazed crowd. Suddenly an engine spark ignited the balloon's inflammable gas and the entire crew was killed.

Airships were then considered unfeasible as a means of making the hazardous journey across the ocean. The dreamers turned to heavier-than-air craft. To spur them on, the London *Daily Mail,* England's largest circulation newspaper, offered fifty thousand dollars to the first aviator to fly the Atlantic nonstop. The offer created a great stir, and the only problem was that there was no plane ready for the trip.

But Glenn Curtiss was working on one. While other inventors restricted themselves to landplanes, Curtiss concentrated on planes that could be usable at sea. His first designs were ordinary planes with pontoons instead of wheels, and he flew the first such plane over San Diego Bay under the watchful eyes of the Navy. His next step was to use rowboat-size hulls instead of the usual fuselage, and again he succeeded.

With remarkable vision, Curtiss foresaw the use of planes in war. Because of his prominence in aviation, he found open doors in Washington where he could plead his case. By the end of 1911, Army, Navy and Marine Corps officers were being sent to San Diego to learn flying from Glenn Curtiss. The first Naval officer to qualify for a Navy pilot license was Lieutenant T. G. Ellyson, who later also became the first pilot to use the catapult as a launching apparatus. The second Navy pilot was Lieutenant John Rodgers. The third was a lean, tense, brown-haired young man with a perpetual frown; his name was John H. Towers. A year after getting his license, Towers set the world's endurance record for hydroplanes by remaining in the air over Annapolis for six hours, ten minutes and thirty-five seconds. A year after that, in 1913, he was assigned as a flying instructor at the Navy's first air station, in Pensacola, Florida.

Glenn Curtiss had taught John Towers how to fly, and the two men grew to be close friends. Whenever he could, Towers visited Curtiss at his seaplane testing grounds at Hammondsport. Often late at night the two young men would sit together and talk about the possibilities of flying across the Atlantic. It was Curtiss who mentioned the idea to Rodman Wanamaker, his East Coast distributor. Wanamaker was immediately captured by the idea and offered to put up the money for Curtiss to build a plane that could make the flight. Lieutenant J. Cyril Porte, a temporarily retired pilot of the British Navy, was then in the United States. He and Towers agreed to co-pilot the ship across the sea.

By the end of July, 1914, Curtiss had the ship near completion. It was called the *America*. It had a wing spread of seventy-two feet and was propelled at first by two 160-horsepower engines—half the power of a modern American car. When the two engines proved insufficient to lift the plane on tests, a third was mounted, providing 480 horsepower. The hull was big enough for a fuel supply, food and two pilots. Everything was set for final tests in August. On August 4, England declared war on Germany and Porte was recalled to duty. There being no safe place to land in Europe, the flight of the *America* was called off. The ship was disassembled and put into storage. Cyril Porte did not forget the *America*. He convinced the British Navy to buy her for patrol duty along Britain's shores. When in 1916 the *America* finally crossed the Atlantic she did so on the deck of a transport.

4

It would only be a matter of time until the United States got into the war. This was the conviction of a clique of rich young amateur mechanics who raced around Long Island in their primitive hot-rods and jazzed-up motorbikes. They talked about it as they loafed around their garages and lounged around the New York Racquet Club. They talked about it, they believed it, but they did nothing. They went into business with their fathers; some of them married and went into business with their fathers-in-law. As often as they could, they got away from their jobs and their homes to work with motors, to play with motors, to talk about motors. Then, on April 6, 1917, the United States declared war on Germany and the young men didn't know what to do with themselves.

They all wanted to be officers. In a way, they were equipped for such duty. All of them were college graduates at a time college graduates were rare. The idea occurred to them of going down to the huge Army training center at Plattsburg and offering themselves en masse for officer's training. But then they heard about the rugged life at Plattsburg, the long hours, the bad food, the red tape, the inevitable mismanagement of the large number of men suddenly dumped upon the Army overnight. They put the idea aside.

One night at the Racquet Club, Amar Johnson said, "Look, I run the Naval National Guard over in Brooklyn. If you fellows really want to get into this war right, why don't you go over to my outfit and enlist and put yourself down for Naval aviation?"

Jim Breese asked, "Well, what on earth is that?"

"It's going to be a big thing," Johnson said, "and when you learn to fly you'll be an officer."

The bait was irresistible.

Larry White glanced up and down the bar. "Who's willing?" he asked.

Jim Breese said, "I am."

Charlie Lawrence said, "I'd like to learn to fly."

Half a dozen others expressed the same inclination. They all piled into Jim Breese's car and drove over to the recruiting office near the Brooklyn Navy Yard and signed up. Their clothes were taken away and they were given sailor uniforms. The recruiting officer said, "Okay, we'll telephone you when we need you." And they all went home.

When Jim Breese entered his house his wife asked, "Are you going to a costume party tonight?"

"I'm in the war," said Breese. "I'm going to be a flying officer."

There was soon considerable doubt about that. Weeks

passed, and none of the Racquet Club Squadron was called to duty. They began to wonder if something had gone wrong, if the Navy even knew they had signed up. They felt foolish running around New York in their sailor suits. Friends who had gone to Plattsburg returned in their neat Army officer uniforms and members of the squadron grimaced every time they were forced to salute the men who had chosen the Army.

Jim Breese said, "I think something's gone wrong. The war will be over before we even get a look at a plane. Maybe I ought to get in touch with Roosevelt."

"Who's he?" Larry White asked.

"Franklin D. Roosevelt, the Assistant Secretary of the Navy."

"You know him?"

"We were at Groton together; we were pretty friendly."

Charlie Lawrence said, "Wait a minute. Let's be careful. If we make the wrong move, we might end up swabbing decks."

Charles Lodge said, "I think the best thing is just to start out on our own."

Breese frowned. "Start our own Navy?"

"Start our training," Lodge clarified. "My father's got a big place out at Bayshore, right on Long Island Sound. Let's go out there and set up camp and get started."

"Who teaches us to fly?" Larry White asked. "The birds?"

Charles Lodge looked toward the door and saw a friend enter. "Him," he said.

The others turned around. Breese asked, "Joe Rutan?"

"Sure," said Lodge. "He can fly. A couple of years ago he went over to Czechoslovakia and taught some Czechs how to fly. Why can't he teach us?"

A week later they were installed on the Bayshore beach. They set up tents. They built an outdoor galley and hired a cook. They chipped in to construct a floating hangar. They had three planes which they borrowed from friends who owned them. Jim Breese knew more about engines than the others and was therefore appointed chief mechanic. Joe Rutan was made flying officer. They were all very busy. They hurried around all day, saluting each other. It was all a lot of fun.

And yet they had the strange feeling that they were not quite with it. They had no contact whatsoever with Washington or the Navy; they were not even getting paid. Worse, they learned that at Huntington, on the opposite side of Long Island, a Wall Street broker had set up a similar aviation camp for his sons and their Yale friends; having unlimited funds, they had acquired numerous planes, publicity and tentative approval of the Navy Department.

Depressed, the Racquet Club Squadron gathered one night for a conference. Breese said, "I still think I ought to get in touch with Roosevelt."

The others were not so sure. Breese had a reputation as a prankster, a buffoon, an indelicate diplomat. By barging into Roosevelt's office, he might do more harm than good. Larry White said, "Charlie Lawrence's family knows some important people in Washington. Charlie, why don't you go down there and nose around before Jim tries his luck at the top?"

It was the movement of a pawn, but the best suggestion at the moment. Lawrence went to Washington. In three days he was back.

"They never heard of us down there," he reported bitterly. "Nobody knows we're out here."

Breese nodded decisively. "Okay. Here's where I go to Roosevelt."

"Not just yet," Lawrence said. "We're going to be inspected."

"Inspected?" said Joe Rutan. "By whom?"

"A lieutenant commander," said Lawrence. "I think his name is Read. The Navy wants to open an aviation training station somewhere on Long Island, so this fellow Read is coming out to inspect us and Huntington."

Charlie Lodge said, "Huntington! What chance do we have against Huntington? They've got a setup like Annapolis."

Lawrence shrugged. "We'll soon find out. Read will be here Thursday."

Larry White moved to the edge of his chair. "There's only one way we can get it," he said. "Huntington has the better setup, admitted, but we're already in the Navy, whether the Navy knows it or not, so all we have to do is be real Navy when this guy Read shows up."

They devised a plan. The road from the Bayshore railroad station forked a half-mile from the beach. One branch ended at the squadron camp; the other ended at a shore point on the opposite side of the twenty-five-foot wide inlet. The Lodge family had dredged the inlet for the convenience of visitors who came by boat.

Larry White said, "I'll get my father's launch and we can put it in the inlet. When Read arrives, we can drive him to the other side, ding the dong as he comes aboard the launch, then bring him across to the camp over water in regular Navy style. That ought to impress him."

Everybody liked the idea. For two days they scrubbed the camp until even the sand glittered. Breese put the three planes in top shape. He also worked on Larry White's boat. It was propelled by a two-cycle engine that was frequently difficult to start. Breese said, "We'd better not take any chances. When I get her running Thursday morning I'll keep her going so that we don't have any trouble when Read gets here."

On Thursday morning, Larry White and Charlie Lawrence drove to the Bayshore station to meet Read's train. They took him directly to the far side of the inlet, where the launch puttered softly and all but one member of the squadron stood at nervous attention. The missing man was Joe Rutan, the best pilot of the group, who was already aloft, with orders to do all the flying tricks he knew.

They were all disappointed at the sight of Lieutenant Commander A. C. Read. He was a small man, just five feet four, and he weighed scarcely 120 pounds. He was hardly the man they had expected to represent the United States Navy. And yet he was one of the best Navy men in the service. He had been near the top of his Annapolis class, he had earned Navy Pilot License Number 43, and he was widely known to be a brilliant navigator. He was Navy to the core. Navy regulations were a religion for him; he worked hard, obeyed orders and kept his mouth shut. He was by birth a quiet man, a New Englander, whose Vermont background had taught him to speak only when it was absolutely necessary, then to say as little as possible. He was reticent, but he seemed curt; he was reserved, but he seemed cold. He was, nevertheless, respected, admired and liked. John Towers had said the Navy had yet to realize his true value. The nickname his classmates had given him revealed their affection for him, although he was a man who showed little affection; he had returned from a summer vacation with no hint of the Northern sun on his face and someone said he looked like putty. Thereafter people called him that.

As he stepped from the car he returned the squadron's salute without looking at the men. He went directly to the launch and stepped down into her. Charlie Lodge dinged the dong. When all were aboard, Jim Breese revved up the engine and guided the launch away from the pier. The engine coughed and spat a few times, then died.

Breese muttered to himself as he leaned over to work on the engine but he could not bring it to life.

They all stood there, blanched with embarrassment and anger, as the launch slowly drifted to the camp shore. The only sound came from Joe Rutan, aloft in a Burgess Dunn, noisily buzzing the beach.

They left the launch as if it were a hearse.

Read worked briskly. He inspected the living tents, the galley, the office, the records, then the hangar, the two planes parked there. He went over the planes carefully. He asked, "Who's in charge of engine maintenance?"

"I am," said Jim Breese.

Read studied Breese for a moment, then nodded almost imperceptibly. "Do you know anything about Liberty engines?"

"What I don't know I can learn mighty quick," said Breese.

Read nodded again. The others frowned at Breese's lack of formal courtesy.

Joe Rutan zoomed low, then banked away. Read pursed his thin lips. "That pilot should be told this is the Navy, not a circus," he said. It was a reprimand; the men knew it.

Read questioned each man about his education, his flight experience and his knowledge of planes. After an hour he announced: "All right, I'm ready to leave."

Larry White said, "We'd be honored if you'd stay for lunch, Commander."

Read glanced at his watch. "I've got to catch the train for Huntington."

Charlie Lawrence said, "We can drive you over to Huntington whenever you want, sir."

"I've already arranged to lunch at Huntington," said Read. They were all disappointed. Well, they hadn't made it. Read's hurry to get away was evidence enough that he was displeased with what he saw. Now what would happen to them?

"All right, sir," Lawrence said. "We'll take you over to Huntington now."

"I can go by train," Read said.

They turned and began to walk toward the inlet. Read stopped and indicated the launch with a nod. "Is there any other way out of here?"

"There's a road to the highway," Larry White said.

"Let's use that," said Read. "It should be safer."

Breese thought he saw a clue of a smile on Read's stoic face, but he was not sure.

The rest of the day passed in misery. They had tried and they had failed. They had failed so badly that undoubtedly their thin thread to the Navy would be cut. Plattsburg, here we come. Friday passed in greater gloom. Early Friday afternoon they all went back to the city and their families. Ordinarily they would have spent some time together over the weekend, but now they avoided each other. A few returned to Bayshore late Sunday night; the others straggled in Monday morning. They were all prepared to break up the camp and go their separate ways.

It was almost noon when Charlie Lodge, waving a telegram, came running down to the beach from his family's house. "We made it!" he shouted. "We made it!" Jolted to life, they all clustered around him as he read:

BROOKLYN NAVY PERSONNEL WILL ARRIVE BAYSHORE IN 48 HOURS TO ASSUME COMMAND, COMMISSION AIR STATION CREW AND BEGIN DESIGNATED FLIGHT TRAINING PROGRAM. LT. JAMES L. BREESE WILL REPORT NAVY DEPARTMENT, WASHINGTON, BY FIRST AVAILABLE TRANSPORTATION TO JOIN LIBERTY ENGINE INSPECTION GROUP UNDER DIRECTION COMDR. RICHARD E. BYRD. BY ORDER ASST. SECRETARY OF THE NAVY, LT. COMDR. A. C. READ.

5

So they were all beginning to find their way to each other: Roosevelt, Taylor, Westervelt, Curtiss, Towers, Byrd, Breese, Read.

II

IN SEPTEMBER, 1917, Admiral Taylor sent for Westervelt and
for Naval Constructor J. C. Hunsaker. The United States
had been in the war for five months; in June, the first American troops had landed in Europe, and they were now waiting for action. On the seas, however, there was a great deal
of action, and the Allies were getting the worst of it. The
German submarine fleet had taken over the Atlantic. No ship
was safe. For over two years, the British had paid heavily
in transports on the race across the sea. Leaving American
ports, each transport tried to make the crossing on its own,
zigzagging north to the Arctic and south to the Equator to
elude the prowling subs. It was a losing battle. The Germans

had only to string a line of U-boats down the middle of the ocean and wait.

The American Navy felt this scatter-shot system was wrong. The results of it were evidence enough. Surely there must be a safer way to get men and supplies across to the battlefields. Thus, when the United States entered the war, the system was changed. Ships left ports in clusters of ten, twenty, even a hundred, always encircled by a barrage of destroyers. In defense, the Navy developed a new weapon: vulcanized cans of TNT. Dropped over the side, the depth charges exploded seconds later and sent out concussion waves strong enough to rip the seams of a submarine. The weapon was improved by the invention of a catapult-type mechanism that could throw the charges hundreds of yards away from the ships, where the subs were more likely to be lurking.

The American system of convoys immediately proved to be far more successful than the British. And yet it was not successful enough. Losses at sea continued heavily.

The price was particularly high in terms of planes. In Europe, the war had moved up into the air, sharply increasing the demand for more and more planes. Most of the planes came from the United States, and most of these from the Curtiss plant. Bulky contraptions, even dismantled, twenty-five of them were enough to fill a transport. When the ship was hit, the loss was immense, not only in itself but especially in the continued lack of air fighters in the European skies. Some way had to be found to overcome the menace.

It was with this in mind that Admiral Taylor summoned Westervelt and Hunsaker to his office. "We've got to get those planes across," he said.

Commander Hunsaker squirmed uneasily in his chair and

frowned. He could bring himself only to nod in uncomfortable agreement. Westervelt said, "You know the problem, Admiral. Those submarines."

"Yes, I do know," said Taylor. "Then we've got to find some way of taking care of those submarines." He picked up a folder on his desk and looked at Hunsaker. "Have you read Westervelt's report on his inspection tour of Europe?"

"Yes, I have. It's not very encouraging. Nobody seems to have any ideas."

The Admiral ran his fingers through his crew cut. "Well, I've still got my idea," he said. "I don't see any other way we can do it." He glanced at both of them. "If we can't get planes over there by sea then we'll have to get them there by air."

Westervelt pursed his lips and his heavy jowls grew thicker. He said, "Admiral, as I reported to you, I've talked this over with the British and the French and they just don't think the plane can be built that can fly the Atlantic."

"What about the *America*, that Curtiss built?" Taylor pointed out.

"He never got it across in the air," said Hunsaker.

"He might have, if the war hadn't interrupted his work," Taylor said. "And we all know she's certainly doing a good job now on patrol duty."

They sat there, the three of them, avoiding each other's eyes. Minutes passed. At last Admiral Taylor said: "I want to go ahead with it." There was a finality in his tone that settled the matter.

Hunsaker asked, "What about Secretary Daniels?"

"I've already discussed it with him and with Roosevelt," Taylor said. "They're leaving the decision to me. They agree with me that the only way we can lick these U-boats is from the air. And you know how I feel. If we can push ahead on the airplane end, it seems to me that the submarine menace could be abated, even if not destroyed, from the air. The ideal solution would be big flying boats that would be able to fly across the Atlantic to avoid the difficulty of delivery. In effect, what we want is a plane that can keep the air and, if need be, keep the sea, too. It must also be able to fight subs and defend itself."

Hunsaker and Westervelt had heard all this before. They watched the Admiral, waiting.

He said, "Go ahead, boys. Build it."

There was nothing more to say.

The two young officers left the Admiral's room. In the corridor they paused and looked at each other. Hunsaker asked, "What do we do now?"

Westervelt said, "I wish I knew."

2

They did two things. They sent a telegram to Glenn Curtiss at Buffalo and asked him to come to Washington as soon as he could. Then they arranged to have Lieutenant Commander Holden C. Richardson transferred from Pensacola to Navy headquarters.

Dick Richardson was then forty years old, and he was widely known as one of the best design engineers in the Navy. At one time he had come close to being deprived of that reputation. In 1897 he had failed in his first attempt to pass the Annapolis entrance examination. He reapplied immediately and spent the next year at his studies. It was then the custom that examinations for both Annapolis and West Point were the same and were given at the same time. In each test area the top scorer was allowed to choose which school he preferred, and the second man had either to accept the remaining school or step aside. In his second attempt, Richardson scored the second highest grade. The top man chose West Point.

As a cadet, Richardson went to Europe on a four-master. Upon graduation, he was assigned to the Bureau of Construction. When the Navy began flight training for its officers, his request for air duty was approved and, like John Towers, he was among the early Navy pilots who received their flying lessons from Glenn Curtiss. During the next half-dozen years he was frequently called in to work on plans for new ships the Navy built—he was particularly skilled in the designing of hulls, but as often as he could he escaped to an air station where he could spend his time at the flying he loved. When he received orders to report to Washington in the autumn of 1917, he had no idea what was expected of him.

Glenn Curtiss was in the same position. He knew only that if the Navy sent for him the subject had something to do with aviation, but whether the Navy wanted more planes or new planes he could not guess. As a precaution, when he left Buffalo two hours after receiving the telegram from Admiral Taylor's office, he took with him W. L. Gilmore and Henry Kleckler, both of his designing staff. They arrived in Washington the following morning by train and went directly to Commander Hunsaker's office. Westervelt was there.

Hunsaker said, "I don't know exactly how to put this, but Admiral Taylor wants a seaplane that can fly the Atlantic."

Gilmore and Kleckler were startled. Curtiss thought for a moment, then asked, "By what route?"

"Who cares?" said Westervelt. "As long as it gets there."

Hunsaker asked, "Can it be done?"

Curtiss looked at him calmly. "Of course it can."

"They don't think so in England and France," said Westervelt. "I've just come back from Europe and I've talked to the best men in aviation there. They say nobody knows how to build a plane that can make such a trip."

"The *America* would have made it, if we'd had more time," said Curtiss.

"That's what Admiral Taylor says," Hunsaker said.

"He's right," said Curtiss, "and he's right about the plane he wants, too."

Westervelt said, "He'll be glad to hear that."

Curtiss asked, "What are the specifications for this plane?"

"The Admiral can tell you that," said Hunsaker. "He's waiting to see you now."

To their own surprise, they found they had little to discuss with Taylor. Even the Admiral had only a slim idea of the kind of ship he wanted. He specified simply that it must be able to fly across the sea and, when it did, it must be usable as a vehicle of war, primarily against submarines. There were two routes such a plane could take: from Newfoundland to Ireland, a distance of some two thousand miles, or from Newfoundland to the Azores, some fifteen hundred miles. Either route would require a sizable ship, if only to hold all the necessary fuel. That was all anybody could be sure of.

Curtiss and his engineers returned to Buffalo that same day. Three days later they were back in Washington with preliminary sketches.

They submitted two designs, one for a plane capable of seventeen hundred horsepower and the other for a thousand. Both were biplanes, with the engines attached to the wing structure; the larger ship would have five engines, the smaller three. A remarkable innovation was the tail. On existing seaplanes, the tail was attached to the hull. In the new design, the tail was held in place by booms from the hull and the superstructure. This, Curtiss pointed out, permitted the use of smaller hulls, and thus decreased the ship's total weight. Another factor was taken into consideration. Up to this time, seaplanes had never flown far enough from shore to present any serious threats to the safe return to their bases, but flying the Atlantic would require many hours over the open seas and the possibility of a forced landing had to be faced. With this in mind, Curtis suggested that the hull should actually be a boat, capable of remaining afloat for a long time. To allow the boat to be more manageable, Curtiss's designs permitted the tail to be easily dismantled and discarded, thereby presenting a less bulky structure to strong surface winds.

Admiral Taylor had no trouble deciding which craft he preferred. Accustomed to dealing with vessels of 200,000 horsepower, he chose the five-engine plane, convinced that the smaller plane was too flimsy to make the trip. The twenty draftsmen in the aeronautics division of the Bureau of Construction immediately went to work on Curtiss's rough designs, and in a few weeks there was some doubt about Taylor's choice. The most impressive planes then in use were the Handley-Page night bombers produced in England. They used two 275-horsepower Rolls-Royce engines and had a lifting capacity of eleven thousand pounds. The seventeen hundred horsepower of Curtiss's big design would have required such a battery of engines that their vibrations would tear any airplane to shreds. Taylor recognized this and changed his mind.

He modified his ideas even further. Originally, he had planned to turn Curtiss's designs over to Navy engineers, then let the Curtiss company construct the plane from final blueprints developed by the Navy. But he realized that the Curtiss staff was far better equipped for the chore than was the Navy. He therefore decided the job could be done better under one roof and turned the entire project back to Curtiss, assigning Navy personnel to work with him in Buffalo.

When Dick Richardson arrived in Washington, he was told of his new assignment of designing the hull of the new plane and he was ordered on to Buffalo.

In December, 1917, Secretary of the Navy Josephus Daniels signed the papers which awarded to the Curtiss Company the contract to build the new planes, which Westervelt had already christened the NCs. The project was now official.

3

They ran into a great deal of trouble. They were pioneers, and like many pioneers they were too ambitious. And they were in a hurry. Rushing, they grabbed at every idea that might make the NC a better plane. During their first weeks of research they found themselves changing the ship's design almost every day. For a while they considered making the NC a triplane because they thought the additional wing space would give the ship greater lift, but then they realized that the power necessary to lift so immense a craft would require too many heavy engines. Always aware of the possibility of ditching, they considered attaching the motors to the hull so that, like the tail, the superstructure could be cast off, thus freeing the hull completely to travel on its own, but they discarded this idea because they could not find room on the hull for all the engines.

At first they agreed on using Rolls-Royce engines, but their subsequent studies revealed that the Rolls-Royce engines were so heavy that the fuel capacity of the NC would have to be cut down to balance out the extra weight. In Detroit, the Ford and Packard motor companies were building Liberty engines for the fighter planes used in Europe. An inspection team headed by Richard E. Byrd and including Jim Breese was in Detroit, assisting the manufacturers. Curtiss knew the Liberty engines were good, but he also knew they lacked the horsepower required for the NC. However, as the NC design was being improved, so were the Liberty engines, and in the spring of 1918 Ford produced a Liberty engine that had more power than the Rolls-Royce and weighed less. The Rolls-Royce engines were rejected.

A parade of couriers traveled constantly between Buffalo and Washington, carrying blueprints of wing beams, ribs, wing struts, tail booms, instrument panels. When the severe Buffalo winter interfered with outdoor work, Curtiss moved the entire operation to Garden City, New York, on Long Island. The parade of couriers continued without missing a step.

There were many arguments. When Dick Richardson took a look at early blueprints, he was appalled by the size of the plane. "A thousand horsepower will never lift this thing," he said. Curtiss engineers argued with him; Navy engineers argued with him; Hunsaker, just back from the National Physical Laboratory of Great Britain, had the latest information on coefficients of resistance, and he argued with Richardson. Everybody labored at drafting boards to prove their points. Richardson was right. The wing spans and over-all length of the NC were reduced accordingly.

Later Richardson lost an argument, this one regarding weight-supporting compression struts. First, Westervelt designed a strut which he called the fishpole because it looked like one; it failed. Then Richardson designed his, which he called the world-beater because of its resemblance to a side paddle on a river boat. He was so sure it would work that he took bets: ice cream sodas. Reluctantly he had to pay off after the first test.

Richardson's major responsibility with the NC was the hull design. The hull was to be both a flight cabin and a boat; therefore it had to be as light as possible and as sturdy as possible; it had to be designed to give the slightest air resistance and to be able to take the severe beating of landing on the high seas, if necessary, at eighty miles an hour.

When Richardson submitted his first designs, fresh battles broke out. Others felt the hull should be made of aluminum; Richardson insisted on spruce. Others felt the hull's length should be proportionate to the plane's immense wing span; Richardson's hull was only forty-five feet, nine inches long, with a beam of ten feet. Objectors said they would feel safer in a peanut shell. In defense, opponents brought over Cyril Porte, who had worked with Curtiss on the *America*. A commander in the Royal Navy and an expert in seaplane design, Porte examined the hull and NC blueprints and declared obliquely: "It is very interesting." And he laughed all the way back to London.

Tests in tanks and wind tunnels upheld Richardson's convictions. Finally the argument boiled down simply to his opinions versus the opinions of his opponents. Endowed with rigid immobility, Richardson won out. He built the hull with his own hands, applying thin layers of spruce to the frame, laminating and reinforcing them with a care and patience that completely unnerved the men who worked with him.

Glenn Curtiss himself disapproved of the hull, and he was most alarmed when Richardson omitted the side fins normally attached to the hull to prevent seaplanes from keeling over in the water. Without consulting the Navy, Curtiss took steps to have the fins put on. Richardson was furious when he learned of this.

"We don't need side fins," he insisted.

"Then how are you going to keep the wing tips out of the water?" Curtiss argued.

"With pontoons."

"Pontoons?"

Richardson took a pencil and hastily sketched a short, sleek pontoon. "These are to be attached to the underside of the lower wing tips," he said. "If for any reason the wings dip, the pontoons will act as a buffer and keep the wing above the water." It seemed plain enough to him.

Curtiss walked away shaking his head.

Others were shaking their heads. In July, 1918, a British Aviation Commission visited the United States and examined the NC as it slowly took shape at Garden City. Colonel Sempill, head of the commission, formally reported:

"The hull of this machine was examined, and is the design of a naval constructor. The machine is impossible, and is not likely to be of any use whatever."

There were many similar observations, from both outsiders and men assigned to build the plane, and yet despite the discouragement no one thought of surrendering the idea. Admiral Taylor was primarily responsible for this. He, after all, had decided that the plane should be built. It was up to him to determine whether the effort should be called off. As criticisms mounted on his desk, he said: "I don't care what other people say about the plane. We've got the best brains in the country working on it. We'll find out soon enough who's been right all along."

Excluding the motors, the cost of one plane was estimated between $50,000 and $75,000, but because of design changes that were continually being made the final cost was almost twice that. The Navy later figured that if the design had been right from the start one ship would have cost about $100,000. When, in January, 1918, the Navy felt ready to begin construction, it was decided to build four of the planes. With the exception of three hulls, the entire contract went to the Curtiss Company. A contract to build two hulls was awarded to Lawley & Sons, Neponset, Massachusetts; the job of building the third hull went to the Herreschoff Manufacturing Company, of Bristol, Rhode Island. Time was important, and to save time the Navy allowed Curtiss to subcontract for the execution of metal fittings, for gasoline and oil tanks, wings, ailerons, nonskid fins, the struts and tail booms, the tail surfaces, the wing-tip floats and the gasoline system valves and fittings. Everybody realized the impossibility of estimating costs accurately, so the budget was left open. Curtiss was permitted to make a 10 per cent profit on the complete job.

Slowly the pieces were put together. From factories throughout the East, parts began to arrive at the Curtiss plant at Garden City. The wing and tail surfaces were made at the Locke Body Company in the heart of New York City, and transporting them the twenty-three miles to Garden City was an engineering feat in itself. Roads between the two points were heavily traveled; it was therefore decided to move the enormous upper outer wing panels—twelve feet wide and over forty-five feet long—at night. The Navy had no trucks big enough to haul the wings and had to rent the massive vehicles normally used to move theatrical scenery around the city.

Lieutenant W. C. Wetherill was in charge of moving the big wings. As the first trip began, he announced: "If anything happens, I'm jumping overboard and I won't bother to come up."

Great care was taken in carrying the wings from the Locke factory to the waiting vehicles. Parts of the building had to be knocked down to get the wings outside. Obstacles on both sides of the street were removed. Red lanterns were hung all over the huge truck as a warning to motorists. Then one car traveled ahead and one behind to wave away oncoming and rear-coming traffic with more red lanterns. Sixty-eight trips were made in this fashion without damage to any parts before the chore was done.

In early August, the actual assembling of the first NC was begun. In view of the constant redesigning that went on, even while various parts were being made, it was remarkable that everything fitted into place. The Liberty engines arrived from Detroit and were tested; they proved excellent.

There was one last-minute setback. One afternoon, Richardson rushed into Westervelt's New York office waving papers and crying: "We've got to change the hull!"

"Change the hull?" Westervelt shouted back at him. "How can we do that at this late stage?"

"We have to. Look." He pointed to the blueprints. "This curve here is going to build up a resistance hump. It'll cut down the lifting power once the plane begins to pick up speed. We'll be lucky to get into the air with 22,000 pounds."

Westervelt sank back in his chair. "Dick, why didn't you think of this before?"

"I just discovered it," Richardson said.

Westervelt said, "People have been criticizing your hull since the day you showed us the plans, but I've backed you every step all the way. Now you're going to make fools out of both of us."

"I can't help that," said Richardson. "We've got to change the hull if we intend to lift that extra weight."

"Well, we can't. It's too late," Westervelt said. "Let's just hope that you're wrong this time."

On September 11, assembled parts of the NC-1 were moved from Garden City to the Naval Air Station at Rockaway Beach. The entire plane was there by September 23, and by the end of the month it was in one piece and ready for testing. A special hangar had been built at Rockaway, intended for all four NCs, but someone had seriously erred in planning its dimensions: the NC-1 filled half the hangar. There could be room for only one more. Embarrassed, the Navy faced the fact that two of the planes, once they were built, would have to remain outdoors.

Marine railways were also built at Rockaway, for launching the planes. Small sixty-horsepower trucks were especially made for pulling the planes from their parking positions to the railway.

On October 1, the Liberty engines on the NC-1 were tested for the first time since their installation, and they worked as well as they had previously. It was then detected that the center of gravity and the center of lift were farther back on the plane than was expected, thus making the ship tail-heavy. To correct this, twelve hundred pounds in sandbags were put in the nose, producing a 16,200-pound over-all weight for the test flights.

Now they were ready.

4

They were afraid to start. So much planning had gone into the giant craft, so much hope, and there had already been so many mistakes that now that the moment of first flight had arrived there was a great wariness in everyone concerned. Because he had been assigned by Admiral Taylor to supervise the actual construction of the plane, Westervelt should have given the order for the test flight and been aboard. Everybody agreed to that. But Westervelt was in Ireland on an inspection trip and nobody knew when he would return. Before leaving, Westervelt had appointed Dick Richardson to command the test flight, in case it was made in his absence. Still fretting about the resistance hump he had detected too late, Richardson was reluctant to give the word that would—or might not—send the seaplane aloft.

They stalled one day, then another. Finally Richardson said: "Well, we might as well find out what we've got here. We go up in the morning."

He sent word to the Curtiss people in Garden City and Buffalo, to the Navy in New York and Washington. Everybody who could make it was at Rockaway the next morning, October 4. At midmorning, the big brass were at the hangar; so were all the personnel of the base. The NC-1 was towed to the railway. Aboard were Richardson, Co-pilot Lieutenant Dave McCulloch of the Naval Reserve, Machinist Philo H. Danly, also of the Reserves, and George Robinson and Van Sicklen, from Curtiss.

Richardson started the three motors. The two outer motors had electric starters; the center motor worked by hand. Then Richardson waved his arm and the holding lines were released and the ship slid into the water.

"Let's get the feel of it," Richardson told McCulloch.

They taxied back and forth in front of the beach crowd several times, getting the touch of the control familiar to their hands. From shore, Danly's head could be seen sticking up from the navigator's cockpit in the bow, his eyes intent on the engines. Just behind the engines Richardson and McCulloch sat in the pilots' cockpit, and about ten feet behind them were the two Curtiss men in the engineers' cockpit. Once more the ship passed the base, then turned again into the west wind, churning up a fierce and narrow wake. The people ashore knew that this was it.

The plane picked up speed. The thirty-six cylinders roared. The wake thinned, then stopped.

The world's biggest seaplane took to the air.

A great cry of triumph rose from the beach.

On her first flight, the NC-1 remained aloft just a few seconds, then settled again in the water. For a moment, the men on the beach wondered if something had gone wrong. Richardson taxied close to the base and sent back word: "Get Captain Parker." Parker, a Coast Guardsman, commanded the Rockaway base and had helped immeasurably in overcoming difficulties of the last-minute work. Richardson said, "Parker should be in on the first ride."

There were half a dozen first rides, each a mere few seconds long. The worries were over, and the base turned into a carnival. Despite all the complaints, criticisms and derisions, the NC-1 could fly, and nobody cared about anything else.

Test flights continued for a month. Several changes were made. The center point still proved to be too far back, so more sandbags were put into the nose. Further changes were made in the electric and fuel systems. Over-all the ship handled beautifully. Even the hump Richardson had worried about failed to appear.

Richardson was ecstactic. "Let's give her a real run," he said. "Let's go down to Washington and show her off to the brass."

At ten-fifty on the morning of November 7, with Richardson and McCulloch at the controls and a crew of seven aboard, the NC-1 took off for Washington. Her total weight was 20,272 pounds—almost the limit Richardson had predicted, and yet she soared into the air after a run of only forty seconds, far better than anyone dared hope.

The plotted course was to take the NC-1 down the coasts of New Jersey and Delaware to Metomkin Bay, then across the peninsula to Chesapeake Bay and up the Potomac to Washington. A half-hour out, the central radiator sprang a leak. Chief Special Mechanic E. H. Howard tried to repair the radiator in flight, but this proved too difficult and Richardson ordered the plane down.

The waves were running ten feet high. Even so, the plane landed without difficulty. Because no one had anticipated problems, there was no water aboard. Howard tried to scoop water from the sea by leaning over the side, but this proved impossible. Being a boat, the hull was equipped with bilge pumps. Howard used one pump to draw water into an ammunition box placed on the deck, then another pump to get the water into the radiator. When repairs were made, take-off was accomplished with only a one-minute run. Nobody realized the important side effects of the incident. Richardson commented that he knew now that his hull definitely was seaworthy, and he was proud of this. One day this fact would save his life.

At five-ten, they were moored at the Anacostia Naval Air Station. Dusk had already fallen. It was too late for the Navy brass to come aboard, and a return flight that day was out of the question. The crew spent the night in Washington, celebrating their magnificent aircraft and the promise it held for American aviation. Next morning, top Navy officials, led by Admiral Taylor, went over to Anacostia for a look at the plane that a lot of people had said should never be built and others had warned would never fly.

After lunch, Taylor accompanied Richardson and the crew to the launch waiting to return them to the NC-1. Taylor said, "All right now, let's get the other three built and put them into action."

A week later the order was revoked. The war had ended. The dangers for which the NCs had been designed no longer existed. The planes were not needed. The years of dreams, the years of hard work, argument and debate, of struggle and finally hope went down the drain.

III

THE FLIGHT to Washington had earned a great deal of publicity for the NC-1—publicity that died as quickly as America's interest in the suddenly ended war. Overnight the military ranks were depleted. Once again, the Army and Navy found themselves in need of recruits. Most men had had quite enough of the armed forces. They shed their uniforms with extreme relief, and their tales of bad food, miserable living accommodations and rigid discipline were enough to convince younger men to look elsewhere for a career. To be sure, the time would come when the veterans would look back on their war experiences as the most adventurous in their lives, a time when they would cling to each other in veterans organizations for the prime purpose of reliving their adventures at rowdy conventions. For the present, however, they were out of uniform and they wanted to stay that way.

There were other things to think about, other topics to fill the headlines. From coast to coast women were organizing to demand the right to vote, and there were strong rumors throughout the land of new laws to prohibit the sale of alcoholic beverages. In the Midwest a teen-age mechanic named Charles Augustus Lindbergh was preparing to enter the University of Wisconsin, aware that his interests were gradually being drawn to aviation.

The Navy's immediate interest was aviation for recruiting purposes. Placards went up in front of post offices urging youth to look to Navy aviation for a career. The Navy hunted for some way to give its campaign a boost.

The boost came from the NC-1. Shortly after the war, a Super-Handley-Page airplane had flown in England with forty passengers, a record. For the sake of publicity, the Navy announced that it would fly fifty people in the NC-1. The flight was made on November 27 at Rockaway and lasted scarcely a minute, but this was enough. When the plane returned to its dock, the passengers were counted and photographed as they disembarked—all of them Navy personnel, which meant home-town publicity for each.

The surprise came when the fifty-first man crawled from the plane. He was Machinist's Mate, Second Class, Harry D. Moulton, who admitted that, disappointed at not being picked for the flight, he had sneaked aboard an hour early and hid among the gasoline tanks. Thus Moulton won the distinction of being the first air stowaway in aviation history.

There were men in the Navy who believed that the NCs

were capable of many aviation firsts. One of them was Commander John H. Towers, one of the Navy's first pilots and a strong promoter of the *America*, which had been sold to England. Towers had spent the war in the United States, in command of flight-training programs, and yet he never put out of his mind the hope of a transatlantic flight. After the war, he was in Washington and in the process of calling on old friends in the Navy Department he visited with Assistant Navy Secretary Franklin D. Roosevelt.

They talked about the flight. Towers pointed out that the NC-1, sitting at Rockaway, had already proved itself. He said, "There are parts of three more NCs in factories all over the country, and they've already been paid for. Why don't we get them to Glenn Curtiss at Garden City and let him assemble them? Then we can make the flight to Europe just for the cost of the gas."

Roosevelt said: "If it were up to me, you could go ahead with it right now. But Joe Daniels is the Secretary. He'll have to make the decision."

"Couldn't you egg him along a little bit?" Towers asked.
Roosevelt smiled. "I can try."

Roosevelt tried for a month. He brought up the idea at staff meetings; he sent regular memoranda to Daniels and to everyone else who might have a voice in the decision. To Navy personnel he wrote in terms of technical achievements and Navy publicity; to politicians he repeated the theme: "Now is the time to build world friendship, and what better gesture than to send peaceful emissaries in American-built aircraft to foreign shores."

Nobody could produce insurmountable objections to the plan. There was, however, a faction of old-timers in the Navy who were reluctant to let the infant aviation division fly off with all the glory, and these were the men who re-

41

placed enthusiasm with caution. Josephus Daniels, influ-enced by Roosevelt's optimism, favored the flight and he spoke of it at cabinet meetings, but during his two terms with the Wilson administrations he had frequent conflict with his own department over decisions which struck the old-timers as too radical. Rather than risk having the old-timers exert pressure against the flight, Daniels went along with their idea that the feasibility of the flight should be studied further. Then Daniels, Roosevelt and Taylor chose the man to make the study. It was Westervelt; there could be no questions about the recommendations of the man who had supervised the construction of the first NC.

But Westervelt was not reckless. He wrote a five-thou-sand-word report, evaluating the flight from every aspect. He began by declaring that the flight was certainly feasible, then went on to outline how it could be done. An important factor was the route. Westervelt estimated than an NC, fully equipped, would weigh about 28,000 pounds. This was a tremendous weight to be held aloft for any great length of time by aeronautic techniques then known. Therefore, a nonstop flight from Newfoundland to Ireland seemed in-advisable. If, however, a North Atlantic route was favored, the planes could go by way of Newfoundland, Greenland and Iceland, but there was the North Atlantic weather to keep in mind. If a southern route were preferred, perhaps stops in South America and Africa would do it. There were, however, the short hops from Rockaway to Newfoundland, Newfoundland to the Azores, the Azores to Portugal. Timed to the good weather—in May, perhaps—this was the best route because the seas would be calm enough to allow for forced landings without serious dangers. In the event of forced landings, Westervelt recommended, Navy destroyers should be spaced all along the Newfoundland-Azores hop to pick up survivors. He also recommended that complete sets of spare parts for each ship be sent ahead to Newfoundland, so that the planes could be repaired, even rebuilt, for the major portion of the flight.

The NC-1, Westervelt pointed out, had just about finished its tests; the NC-2 was near completion when the end of the war stopped work on it—it could be readied quickly; the NC-3 could be ready in February and the NC-4 in March. Westervelt recommended that all four ships make the trip to Newfoundland, then the best three could attempt the flight to the Azores. Westervelt felt chances were better than two to one that two of them would make it, three to one that one might.

He submitted his report to Captain John P. Tompkins, Navy Operations, on January 15, 1919. Two days later, the NC-1 was declared ready for active duty and assigned to Rockaway. On February 4, Tompkins, Towers and Lieutenant Commander G. D. C. Chevalier sent a follow-up report to J. S. McKean, Acting Chief of Naval Operations, recommending endorsement of Westervelt's suggestions. McKean endorsed the plan and sent it on to Secretary Daniels. Daniels approved it the same day.

The flight was on.

2

Up to this point, discussions and reports regarding the flight were classified as secret. As final plans were being developed, the London *Daily Mail* renewed its offer of fifty thousand dollars to the first pilots to fly the Atlantic, an offer previously withdrawn when the war broke out, and it was known that the British government was extending its co-operation to English fliers interested in making the try. Because of this, Tompkins, Towers and Chevalier recommended that the British government be informed of the Navy's plans. They concluded their report with:

In view of the fact that the only logical point for the beginning of the flight is a port in Newfoundland, which is a British Colonial port, and in view of the possibility that Great Britain contemplates an expedition of this nature at about the date recommended above [May], an awkward situation may result from the independent preparations being carried out by the two countries at the same port. In order to avoid any complications of this nature and also in view of the fact that the United States and Great Britain have cooperated to a great extent in the development of the latest types of seaplanes, which has made this project practicable, it is recommended that information regarding the proposed flight be furnished the proper British authorities; and it be suggested to them that if they contemplate an expedition of this nature, arrangements be made to start both expeditions simultaneously, in order that the patrols and other facilities may be utilized conjointly.

In view of the important role being taken by the United States in international affairs and of the necessity of avoiding any possibility of giving offence to any of the great nations with which we are associated, attention is invited to the desirability of supplying information in regard to this flight to governments of France and Italy also, in order that both or either of these countries may have planes to participate if desired. It is believed that the prestige obtained by the United States Navy in thus initiating and making possible a great international flight of this nature will equal or exceed that obtained by attempting the flight alone and all chance of international jealousies will be avoided.

But the admirably diplomatic suggestions were wasted. The day Secretary Daniels approved the flight plans, special orders were issued, naming Towers as commander of the flight. In the rush of activity, somebody forgot to label the

44

orders "secret," and they were posted in the Navy Department with other assignment orders. Alert newspapermen, examining the orders, came upon Towers's name and saw the words "in connection with preparation for Trans-Atlantic flight," and that was all they needed to rush Daniels for further details. Daniels held a press conference and told the whole story.

The story hit front pages around the world. From official sources abroad came cool wishes for good luck. What looked like belated efforts to make the flight an international endeavor were received in the same spirit. Whether it wanted to or not, the American Navy was faced with the single choice of going it alone. Civilian pilots—particularly British —took a different stand. Resentfully, they accused the Navy of using its superior facilities to cop the *Daily Mail's* fifty-thousand-dollar prize. Repeatedly the Navy assured that its flight would be strictly scientific, that it was not interested in the prize money and would not allow its personnel to accept it.

Nevertheless, there was no doubt about the Navy's anxiety to be the first to fly the Atlantic. Westervelt's estimate that the four NCs could be ready by March was a slight exaggeration. The Three and Four were nowhere near ready; they had not even left the drawing boards. To make up for the lost hours caused by the postwar slowdown, the Navy went to work overtime. Men at Garden City and Rockaway worked past midnight every day, including Sundays.

Ideas for further innovations were proposed. Radios were installed on the planes, the first to be used in aviation. Short-beam radios allowed for contact between the planes and the destroyer lookout ships. For long-distance wireless, 250-foot antennas on reels were attached to the lower wings; the antennas were extended and cranked in by hand.

Two important gadgets were produced by Lieutenant Commander Richard E. Byrd. In addition to his work in Detroit with Liberty engines, Byrd had been appointed commander of the Navy base at Nova Scotia from which small planes hunted German submarines off the coast. His experiences at blind flying in bad weather brought to light several serious navigational problems the NCs would face, and he solved them.

The major problem was the air drift caused by strong winds. The navigator on a surface ship had instruments to determine drifts, but pilots did not. A simple compass was useless because it did not take drift into consideration: it could point in the right direction but still not indicate the drift off course. Also, the surface navigator could establish his exact position with the use of a sextant, that ancient mariner's instrument by which he could "shoot" the sun or stars against the horizon and thus compute his location with great accuracy. But existing sextants would be of no help to a pilot who was in a fog or above the clouds where he could not see the horizon. For that matter, even in clear weather a pilot did not have a true horizon because of the curvature of the earth. Obviously new instruments were needed to account for drift and the false horizon at high altitudes.

Dick Byrd overcame both problems by designing new instruments to meet them. His aerial sextant used a bubble, exactly like a carpenter's level, and thus created a false horizon. Even if the plane was at an angle, the sextant could always be level in relation to the stars. As the sun, moon and stars were always in known fixed positions for each moment of the day or night, the air navigator could fix his position as accurately as a ship's captain. Byrd also invented a wind-and-drift indicator: by dropping to the water a flare bomb at night or an oil patch by day, then measuring with a special indicator the speed with which they drifted on the surface, the air navigator could determine the velocity of the wind that was pushing his plane off its course either to the left or right and make adjustments. One Sperry invention was the turn-and-bank indicator, again based on the bubble principle. It enabled pilots flying blind to determine whether or not they were flying level and to make corrections.

When Byrd learned of the proposed NC flight, he hurried to Washington and offered his inventions for use on the transatlantic effort. They were accepted. He also offered himself, but he was rejected.

Ordinarily, Byrd, because of his position and experience, would have been placed in command of one of the NCs, but the Navy had decided that the crews would be composed of men who had not seen overseas duty during the war. Byrd's service in Nova Scotia excluded him; he was to go only as far as Newfoundland for the testing of his inventions. Jack Towers, in making up his crew lists, felt that most of the men could come from the personnel at Rockaway, but he wanted the best available men for the key positions. He chose Richardson and McCulloch because of their past experience with the NC-1. He sent for Jim Breese because of his knowledge of Liberty engines. The ship commanders would also be the navigators, and Towers reached across the country for the most capable men.

He chose Lieutenant Commander Marc Mitscher as skipper of the NC-2. Mitscher had bilged out of Annapolis after two years, but his father managed to wangle a second appointment for him. Mitscher was an impossible student, who didn't care for the discipline, the hazing, the study or anything else. How he managed to graduate, to be chosen for the NC flight, then subsequently become a hero of the Pacific in World War II long remained a mystery to his closest friends. But he was a brilliant pilot and he possessed great creative insight. It was this instinct which helped him solve one of the NC problems that persisted to the last minutes of flight preparations. The heavier the ships were loaded, the more uncertain their take-offs became. The planes already had three engines. To add a fourth in front of the wings would require wholesale redesign of the planes, so that was out of the question. Mitscher thought it over, then suggested: "Why not put the fourth engine behind the other three as a pusher instead of a puller?" Nobody had thought of that before. It was tried, and it worked.

Towers selected the NC-3 as his flagship, with Richardson and McCulloch as his pilots. In command of the NC-1, he put Lieutenant Commander Patrick N. L. Bellinger. Tall, handsome, blond, Bellinger, at thirty-four, held the Navy's Number 8 pilot license. He also held the U.S. altitude record for seaplanes, at ten thousand feet. Another of his distinctions was the fact that he was the first Naval aviator to be shot at in combat—during the Mexican border wars.

Towers knew that probably the best air navigator in the Navy was Putty Read. Read had ended the war at a desk job in Washington. Towers was aware that Read's wife—Bess Burdine, whose family owned the biggest department store in Miami—was expecting a child, and he suspected that Read might not want to be away from home at this time. But Towers also realized that quiet, sober-faced Read was a "book" sailor, who did what he was told and never questioned an assignment. Towers preferred that Read himself should make the decision and he wrote a friend in Navy Personnel to sound Read out.

The man walked down the corridor to Read's office, poked

his head in the door and asked: "Hey, Putty, you wanna fly one of the NCs to Europe?"

Read said: "Okay."

"You're on."

3

Read arrived at Rockaway on Friday, April 25, to take command of the NC-4. The plane had come off the production line a week earlier and had yet to be flown. While the final work was being done, Read devoted himself to the study of Byrd's instruments and to his sea charts. He practiced so much that he could plot his position in half, often a third, of the time the other navigators required.

The excitement which the NC-1 flight to Washington caused had long since faded. The flutter of interest upon Towers's appointment had dimmed. The Navy was moving too slowly to satisfy reporters, and even the long hours of activity at Rockaway failed to hold their attention. Instead, attention was focused northward, on Newfoundland, where ten teams of British fliers had gathered to compete for the fifty thousand dollars. There seemed little doubt in the public's mind that the first men to fly across the Atlantic would be British. The papers were full of them. Two teams were favored: Fred Raynham and Bill Morgan; Harry Hawker and Harry Grieve. Only bad weather kept them from hopping across to Ireland. On the far side of the sea, bad weather held back the R-34 dirigible from trying a westward crossing.

These were the men whose names filled the papers, and thus there was no report that, on April 14, Assistant Navy Secretary Franklin D. Roosevelt traveled to Rockaway to inspect the NCs personally. Secretary Daniels was in Europe with President Wilson, which was all to the good. Among the top Navy civilian officials, it was Roosevelt who did most to bring the NCs close to their moment of departure. During the last months of preparation, Roosevelt had discovered that Jim Breese, his boyhood friend, was going on the trip, and he offered: "Jim, if there is anything I can do to hurry things along, let me know."

"You can do plenty," Breese said. "We're going through an awful lot of red tape to get the money we need to buy parts."

Roosevelt said, "I have authority to approve purchase orders up to a thousand dollars. When you need more than that, just ask me twice."

At Rockaway, Roosevelt was as excited as a schoolboy. "I want to go for a ride," he told Towers.

Towers looked at the sky. "It looks pretty rough up there."

"I won't mind. I want to go up."

He went up in the NC-3, piloted by Richardson and McCulloch, sitting in a special chair installed for him directly behind the fliers. The flight lasted just fifteen minutes, and it was a rough and bumpy trip. Towers worried about Roosevelt, but when Roosevelt came ashore again he was only slightly pale and all smiles.

"She's wonderful, Jack," he said. "You'll have a glorious trip. I wish I could go with you."

Towers was beginning to wonder if he would be going himself. There had been a lot of trouble. In February, the NC-1, while on the handling platform, was hit by gale winds that tore the control column loose and damaged the plane. A few days later, the NC-2 was roaring across the bay on a take-off when a smaller plane, fifteen hundred feet up and at target practice, dropped a 250-pound depth charge at a marker. The barrel of death crashed into the bay just 150 feet from the NC, jarring everybody aboard and killing the engines. Then, in March, the NC-1 was again hit by gale winds, this time while she was moored in the bay. The wings on one side were ruined. The NC-2 had been acting badly; since there was no time to have new wings made, nobody particularly minded cannibalizing the NC-2 wings— nobody, that is, except Marc Mitscher, who thus lost his command. Towers assured him a place on the trip by making him first pilot of the NC-1.

Troubles persisted to the last moment. On May 1, the scheduled date of departure, severe storms hit the East Coast, forcing a postponement. Then the hangar fire broke out, damaging the One and Four. Again the NC-2 provided the spare parts. Then, just a few hours before take-off, Chief Special Mechanic Howard got in the way of a Four propeller and lost his hand. That night Towers told the few reporters at Rockaway that the flight was again indefinitely postponed; the next morning he changed his mind and announced immediate take-off.

It was, therefore, a glum group of men who assembled outside the hangar on the gray morning of May 8 to hear their orders read for the last time, to shake hands and say good-by to the Rockaway commanders and to accept four-leaf clovers from Captain Irwin.

Towers ordered, "Board your craft."

The group broke up into crews and headed for their planes. Then Jim Breese had a sudden thought. He said aloud, "Where's the head?"

Everybody stopped and looked at him.

Breese said: "I just thought of it. We're going to be aboard these things for a long time and they've got no heads. Where do we go?"

Here was something else everybody had overlooked: the planes had no toilets. A Rockaway ensign said, "Just a minute." And he dashed off in the direction of the supply house. He was back almost immediately, equipped with an armful of assorted weather balloons. "These should do," he said.

They all laughed, softly, almost sadly. They went to the ships and climbed aboard. In less than five minutes the three massive planes had slid down their railways and roared out into the bay.

IV

JIM BREESE had a headache. He was huddled in the rear cockpit of the NC-4 with Chief Machinist Eugene S. Rhoads, who had replaced the injured Howard. Breese said, "We shouldn't have gone out last night, Smokey."

The noise of the engines was too great. Rhoads shouted, "What, sir?"

They were banking left, on the tail of the Three, falling into line to pick up the southern shore of Long Island. Behind, rising from the bay to join them, came the NC-1. Breese pointed at his head and shook it. "Last night," he said. He made a gesture of drinking from a bottle. "That cheap booze," he said, and shook his head. "We shouldn't have done it." He pointed now to the roaring engines and shook his head again to indicate the pain they were giving him.

Rhoads looked smug. He felt no aftereffects of the previous evening. "I was going to bring a bottle along, but I threw it out instead."

Breese shuddered and turned his face away.

They were all up now, at five hundred feet, in a neat V formation, four hundred yards apart, with Towers leading in his flagship, Bellinger's One on the right flank and Read's Four on the left, all of them eager to make a good showing as they passed over the base.

Rhoads leaned over the side and studied the cluster of upturned faces of the base personnel. He waved cheerily at them. "I give you all a Navy salute," he shouted. "Drop dead!"

Breese made no comment, but his silent disapproval was tinctured with amusement. He shook his head again. "I should know better than to fraternize with enlisted men."

Up forward in the navigator's cockpit at the nose of the ship, Putty Read was busy with Byrd's instruments, already taking quick readings. Satisfied, he reached for the logbook at his feet. It was an ordinary ledger, alphabetized down the right edge. During the last preflight days he occupied himself one evening numbering the pages; he got to ninety-one, then stopped. On the page marked with the printed "A" he wrote: "Note Book—TransAtlantic Flight, May, 1919—A. C. Read, USN—Commanding Officer and Navigator of NC-4." At the page marked "B" he listed his crew, then he made crisp daily entries from May 3 to May 7, commenting on delays caused by weather and accidents. Beginning on pages 13 and 14 and on alternate sets of pages thereafter as far as he had numbered, he entered the dozen different technical matters he would be recording in flight—fuel supplies, water supply, visibility, drift, speed, altitude, engine behavior.

Now they were in flight. Read picked up the book, took the stub of a pencil from his pocket and turned to page 15. The plane was vibrating badly, making his hand shake. He glanced at his watch, set to Greenwich Mean Time,* and he wrote:

> Took off at 2:02
> Left Rock. 2:09
> Clearing gradually at Montauk Pt. Sun came out.

2

Jack Towers saw the sun and nodded at it approvingly. Weather had held them back: he wanted no more trouble with weather. The ships would be trouble enough. The flight to Halifax amounted to a shakedown cruise, and if anything was going to go wrong with any of the aircraft he wanted it to happen now while they were all in sight of land. His own plane was behaving well enough. He turned to Dick Byrd, squeezed beside him in the navigator's cockpit, and gave him an inquiring grin.

---

* G.M.T. is known variously as Greenwich Meridian Time, Greenwich Mean Time or Greenwich Time. This indicates the starting point from which standard time is reckoned throughout the world.

The earth turns on its axis once every 24 hours. By dividing the earth into 24 imaginary time zones extending from the North to South Poles, each zone would be a 15° segment representing a time difference of one hour. (The U.S.A. has four time zones, Canada, seven.)

The universal starting point is Greenwich, England, because of the Royal Observatory built there in 1675 for the advancement of navigation and nautical astronomy.

The United States adopted the system in 1883; it was made necessary by the great railroads traveling across the country and the need for a standard time schedule.

Byrd returned the grin, then leaned to Towers's ear and said, "Wonderful."

Towers nodded again. Then he ducked into the hull and made his way bent over to his radioman, Lieutenant Commander R. A. Lavender. "Get reports," he said. He returned to his cockpit.

Lavender tapped out the flight's code name on his wireless, then added: "Report."

The One answered first. Lieutenant (jg) Harry Sadenwater replied: "Skipper says all well." From the Four, Ensign Herbert C. Rodd sent: "Everything under control. Read."

Lavender scribbled the reports on small pieces of paper and took them forward. Standing in the cockpit with his head and shoulders exposed to the roaring wind, Towers did not hear Lavender address him. Then he felt a tap on his legs and looked down.

"The reports," Lavender said.

Towers took them, read them, inserted them into his logbook.

They were over Montauk Point at noon. At this point, their flight plan specified a north turn, with Block Island as the next landmark. Already the island was in sight, and beyond it, far ahead, lay the dark haze of the New England coast. Towers plotted the change in course and sent the new compass reading to Richardson and McCulloch at the controls, at the same time instructing Lavender to notify Read and Bellinger. The three planes pivoted northward in a wide sweep that caused Bellinger to slip back out of formation. Read saw that the turn had broken up the neat triangle they had maintained since Rockaway, and he shook his head impatiently; he disliked untidiness.

"Come on, Pat," he muttered. "Catch up."

Bellinger could not possibly have heard him, and yet the One seemed to tremble excitedly and surge ahead in eager obedience.

They passed over Block Island at twelve-fifteen, all of them at approximately two thousand feet. The island looked like a picture postcard sharply photographed. They could clearly see the surf breaking on the beaches, the houses, the roads and fields, the mainland steamers with their stubby streams of smoke. Over the island they set their course for Vineyard Sound.

The air crackled with radio messages from land and ship stations, reporting the flight's movements. At about twelve-thirty, Lavender heard his own call letters and acknowledged. It was the Chatham Navy Base calling, with a message for Towers. Lavender took it down, then crawled through the flagship to Towers and gave it to him. It read:

DELIGHTED WITH SUCCESSFUL START. GOOD LUCK ALL THE WAY. ROOSEVELT.

Towers noted the message in his log.

Updrafts from the islands and a brisk northwest wind created a turbulence that sent the three planes into a series of severe bumps. In the rear cockpit of the Four, Smokey Rhoads suddenly acquired a sour taste in his mouth and for a moment he thought he was going to vomit. He made a move to slide down into the hull, but stopped when he looked below and saw Putty Read working his way aft.

Read caught Rhoads's eye and motioned to him. He said, "The intercom isn't working. I can't contact the pilots from my cockpit."

"I'll check it, sir," Rhoads offered, and he moved away.

Read looked after Rhoads quickly, wondering whether his voice had sounded a bit odd. He decided not to find out: there was no sense in looking for trouble—he had enough already. He turned to Radioman Rodd. "Notify the flag that I'd like to increase speed until we get out of this bumpy area. It's like riding a camel, up forward."

Rodd said, "Aye, aye, sir." And he sent the message.

Read then went to the pilots' cockpit and hoisted himself up until his small head appeared at Walter Hinton's knees. Hinton was surprised to see his commander's head come up through the floor openings, then leaned forward.

Read said, "The intercom is broken."

Hinton said, "Oh? I hadn't noticed."

Read nodded, then: "I've asked for permission to increase speed."

"Yes?"

"If it's okayed, watch me for hand signals."

"Okay, Putty."

"Everything okay here?"

"Fine."

Read was about to return to the hull when Rodd handed him a radio message. "FLAG TO COMMANDERS: PROCEED AT WILL BUT REMAIN WITHIN RADIO RANGE." Read passed the note to Hinton, who read it, then gave it to Co-pilot Elmer F. Stone.

Read said, "Take her down to fifteen hundred feet, then open her up for a while."

When Bellinger was handed the same message by Radioman Sadenwater, he looked around just in time to see the Four begin to surge ahead. He clicked on his intercom. "Navigator to pilots."

Marc Mitscher replied, "Yes, Pat?"

58

"The flag has turned us loose, Marc. Want to give Putty a race?"

Mitscher lifted himself in his seat and saw the Four, now passing the flagship. "He's got a good lead."

"Let's try," Bellinger said.

Mitscher told Co-pilot Lou Barin, "Let's see what she can do." The NC-1 engines gulped at the spurt of fuel and lunged forward with a jolt.

Read had no idea a race was on. At the lower altitude and greater speed, the Four rode smoother, and this was all he had wanted. Over Vineyard Sound, Read figured he had moved ahead of the flagship a bit more than he should, so he raised his right arm and waved it in a circle. Hinton understood the gesture and made a complete, wide left turn, bringing the Four back into position to port and astern of the Three. As the plane took its place, Bellinger's craft roared by overhead and moved into the lead. Read watched it go and wondered what in the world was going on. Had there been additional instructions from the flag? He peered into the cabin to see if Rodd had messages for him, but the radioman gave no such indications.

They passed over Woods Hole and now, according to the flight plan, were to make for Monomoy Point. Once again they hit bumps. Read's navigation instruments jiggled in his hands as he took a quick reading. Something was wrong. He looked ahead and saw that the other two planes were traveling in a sharper northerly direction than he was. He turned around and motioned to his pilots to follow them, but there was no reaction. Annoyed, Read left his cockpit and went to the pilots.

"Hinton, what are you doing? We're off course," he said.

"I thought you wanted to avoid the bumps," said Hinton.

"Yes, but we have to stay on course."

Hinton shrugged and let the criticism pass. "Aye, aye," he said.

Read returned to the ship's nose and noted crisply in his log: "Found pilot was steering a course of his own. I heaved to port to gain distance to north and pass near Elizabeth Island."

By one-thirty, they had all passed Monomoy Point and were out over Nantucket Shoals. There was a slight haze, but Massachusetts Bay was clear and they could see Cape Cod. Now the course was changed to make for Cape Sable, on the southern tip of Nova Scotia. This was actually the start of the overseas flight: they would soon be out over the open waters, with only the patrol ships to mark their course. The idea that they were on their way at last sent a shiver of excitement through every man on the three planes.

In a few minutes they were out of the sight of land and the haze closed in on them. Bellinger had given up his race as soon as he realized Read was not in on it; he instructed Mitscher to let the One slow down, then bring her abreast and to port of the flagship. The two planes were almost side by side when Jack Towers spotted the first patrol ship, the *McDermot*, dead ahead, sending up a heavy smoke as a signal of identity.

Towers called his radioman on the intercom. "Lavender, we're about to pass over the *McDermot*. Send her an acknowledgment and thank her for standing by."

"Aye, aye, sir."

Satisfied, Towers glanced over at the One, neatly pacing him. Bellinger's head, popped over the navigator's cockpit, some five hundred yards away, looked like a button. Towers picked up his binoculars and beamed them at Bellinger and saw, to his mild surprise, that Bellinger was watching him through binoculars. Towers waved; Bellinger waved back.

"Now," said Towers, "where the devil is Putty?"

3

The NC-4 was more than ten miles behind, and she was in trouble. Haze and distance had put the two sister ships out of sight. Repeatedly since leaving Cape Cod, Read had turned around to his pilots and waved them on, to increase speed, but they had not responded. He had the uneasy feeling that somebody was dragging his feet. He was not worried about getting lost or being abandoned, but he knew that the ship's radio was unreliable, fluctuating without warning from as much as a hundred miles to less than five, and he did not want to wander beyond range in the event of any sudden change in plans.

He turned around again and waved at Hinton and Stone. "Come on," he shouted over the wind, "let's move."

Nothing happened. Read cursed the intercom for being broken, and he was about to leave his cockpit to go aft and find out what was wrong when he felt a tug on his pants' leg. He lowered himself into the cabin.

Jim Breese was worried. "The after-center engine is out, Commander," he said. Despite their weeks of working together, Breese could not bring himself to familiarity with Read; Read's New England crispness, his severe Navy bearing and the fiasco of inspection day at Bayshore two years before all combined to discourage it.

Read asked, "What happened?"

"The oil pressure is down to nothing and the spark has cut out," said Breese.

"When did this happen?"

61

"The pressure's been dropping for about ten minutes," Breese said. "She conked out just now. I reported to you right away."

Read crawled back into the navigator's cockpit and looked aft at the engines. Yes, the after-center was dead, all right. He returned to Breese. "Where's the machinist mate?"

Breese thumb-pointed over his shoulder. "He's air-sick."

Read looked aft and saw Smokey Rhoads stretched out on the deck.

Read remembered his momentary misgiving about Rhoads of just a while ago. "Did he check out the engines before take-off and report to you?"

"Yes, sir."

Breese smiled inwardly, remembering Rhoads's earlier cockiness.

Read glanced at Rhoads's recumbent figure. Well, what could you expect? A new man who had been brought in at the last minute; probably knew his business well enough but perhaps overwhelmed by the excitement of flying the Atlantic. Read blamed himself for not checking out every inch of the ship himself before leaving Rockaway.

He beckoned to Herbert Rodd. "Notify the flag that we've lost our after-center engine. We'll try to keep up but we won't expect the others to wait for us."

Rodd turned to his radio.

Read told Breese, "Tell the pilots to keep their eyes on me. I can't be running back here every two minutes." He looked at Rhoads again.

He returned to his cockpit and saw the smoke of the *McDermot* well off to port. He raised his left arm and pointed. Stone and Hinton understood the gesture and veered the Four to the left, banking until Read's arm pointed straight ahead. They passed directly over the destroyer, squarely on course.

They were losing altitude, but Read was not concerned. Three engines could keep the plane aloft. Although they would certainly lose speed, they ought to be able to reach Halifax, late, surely, but in time to make repairs before the next hop, to Newfoundland.

The *McDermot* passed out of sight. For a moment, Read got a glimpse of the One and Three farther ahead. He allowed himself to relax a bit and occupied himself with the course. Some fifty miles farther north was the second pilot ship, and Read wanted to be able to cross directly over her without last-minute darts to correct drifts.

They went on for ten miles, then twenty, then twenty-five, holding their altitude at approximately fifteen hundred feet. From time to time, Read looked up at the three remaining engines, a hint of hope in his impatient eyes. Suddenly he felt rain strike his head and arms. He looked up: the sky was clear. Puzzled, he turned back and sent an appraising study at the engines. Erupting from the forward-center engine was a shower of water and steam. Suddenly he saw a connecting rod arc lazily into the ocean. A second engine was out. The plane began to drop rapidly.

Read rushed into the cabin. He shouted to Rodd, "Notify the flag that we're making a forced landing." Then he hoisted himself up between the two pilots.

There was heartbroken disappointment on Stone's face. Hinton said, "Rotten luck, Putty."

"Take her down," said Read. "We're going to have to ditch. Can you handle her?"

Hinton nodded, uncertain. "We may hit hard. I can't tell from here how the seas are running. But we'll handle her."

Read let himself slide back into the hull, landing at Breese's feet. Breese said, "Commander, we're jinxed!"

Smokey Rhoads began to stir. Read pointed sternly at him and ordered, "Get ready to land."

Rhoads asked unsteadily, "Are we there?"

"Shut up, Smokey," Breese said. "Let's get back to the rear."

Rodd stepped up. "The flag has acknowledged. The McDermot, too. We're to give our position as soon as we land and they'll send a ship to pick us up."

"All right," Read said. "Get ready."

Breese and Rhoads went to the rear cockpit and strapped themselves in. Rodd fastened the belt at his radio equipment. Read returned to the forward compartment and watched the sea come up at him. At a thousand feet he could see the maze of whitecaps, but it was impossible to estimate the waves. At five hundred feet he could judge that the sea was rough. At one hundred he decided he'd better get out of the bow. He ducked inside just as the plane struck.

4

Within minutes after the distress signal, Towers, the McDermot and the Chatham Navy Base relayed the message to Rockaway, to New York and to Washington. The Kimberly, the second station ship, radioed that the One and Three had passed over her, but she had not seen or heard the Four. The Atlantic Fleet commanders presumed Read had gone down between the two destroyers. Vessels Boston and Chatham began to steam up to begin a search. Roosevelt instructed from Washington: "All ships in North Atlantic ports will commence search for missing NC-4. Station ships along flight route will join search immediately after remaining aircraft pass over. Air station commanders will assign available planes to search until further orders."

Jack Towers was worried. Crammed into the navigator's cockpit with Dick Byrd, he observed, "Putty's wife is going to have a kid."

"Don't worry about Putty," Byrd said. "If his plane was still in one piece two minutes after she ditched, Putty will keep her that way." Byrd looked back at his navigation instruments.

"I'd hate to have anything happen to him," said Towers. "I personally picked him for this flight; I'm responsible for him."

"He'll be all right." Byrd tried to move in the tight compartment. "Jack, I want to check the drift." He was a boy preoccupied with a toy he had made himself.

Towers left the cockpit and made his way into the cabin, pausing at the radio table and leaning over Lavender's shoulder. "Any news on Read?"

"They're all out looking for him."

"Anybody heard from him?"

"No, sir."

"You think maybe his radio was knocked out?"

"Maybe. These battery sets don't have much range at all at sea level. Maybe that's it: he can't reach anybody."

Dick Richardson turned the controls over to Dave McCulloch and came down into the cabin. "Have they found Read?"

"Not yet," Towers said.

Richardson made a pleading study of the hull that surrounded them. "It should be able to take it," he said, more to himself. "It's a good hull. It should be able to take it."

"I hope so," Towers said.

Richardson raised his heavy brows hopefully. "Dave and I landed in rougher weather on the Washington flight, and the hull took it then," he said. "She's a good boat, Jack. I put everything I know into her. It all depends on how hard they hit. Dave and I had full control when we ditched. But did Read?"

Towers said, "That little guy never lost control of anything, even himself."

"Yes," said Richardson, understanding.

Towers asked Lavender, "How's the One?"

"Purring right along," Lavender said. "Lieutenant Sadenwater reported in a few minutes ago." He handed Towers a piece of paper; Towers glanced at it and returned it. Lavender added, "He said they'd be standing by for landing instructions."

Towers looked at his watch, then at Richardson. "Another couple of hours?"

"About that. We're running into headwinds."

Towers told Lavender, "Tell them we'll instruct them later, about fifteen minutes out. And let me know if you hear anything about Putty."

"Yes, sir. I'm in constant touch with the station ships; they'd most likely hear it first."

It was almost five o'clock. Towers rejoined Byrd in the bow. Byrd pointed ahead to a dark line growing on the horizon. "Cape Sable," he said. "Right on the button. If this wind holds out, I figure Halifax in exactly two hours."

Again they were right on the button. They sighted Halifax at a quarter to seven, New York time, slightly less than nine hours out of Rockaway. The distance of 540 nautical miles had been flown at a consistent sixty knots an hour, the longest overwater flight at the best overwater speed. They came in long and low over the harbor, Towers first,

Bellinger ten minutes behind by prearrangement. The Three took the water squarely off McNab's Island, then made for the town of Eastern Passage, where American fliers had been stationed during the war. Small boats clustered around the big plane as she roared ahead, high in the water. A big crowd had come down from Halifax to welcome her. The One circled overhead, waiting until the Three was moored and her crew had gone ashore, then she came in to receive her own tributes.

The Mayor of Halifax was there, the American Consul, and every newspaperman who could reach the place. They all crushed around Jack Towers, shaking his hand, pounding his back, storming him with questions.

He was suddenly very tired. He asked, "Is there any news of Commander Read?"

5

Jim Breese had spent two hours atop the Four's hull trying to repair the damaged engines before he gave up. Rather than put the blame on anyone, Read recorded that the trouble had started when certain oil pipes chilled at high altitudes and that the oil had been lost when the forward engine cracked.

Read asked Rodd, "Can you contact anybody?"

"No, sir. I can hear a lot of them. They're all talking about us, but nobody seems to be listening for us." Rodd tapped his battery set impatiently. "I doubt if we're getting more than a mile or two out of this thing now."

It was five o'clock. Read said, "Let's see if we can find our way back by ourselves." He went into his cockpit and took a reading: they were about eighty miles from the nearest shore, twenty miles farther than Read had expected.

He summoned Stone. "We might as well try to taxi in,"

he said. "It'll be getting dark soon. There's no sense sitting here waiting."

"All right, sir," Stone said. He looked at the sea. "It shouldn't be too bad."

They had landed in a ten-foot sea, settling on the crest of a wave with surprising ease. Then, just as they exhaled with relief, a second wave hit them with bullet force, making the whole ship tremble. They waited, afraid. A third wave struck, sending water through the hatches and drenching all of them. For perhaps a hundred yards they bobbed along from crest to crest, at last slowing enough to slide down the side of one wave and up the side of another. When they got used to the severe rhythm and when they were confident that the hull would hold, they relaxed and went to work.

On command from Read, Stone started the two outer engines and they began to head west. Read himself served as lookout in the forward cockpit; Breese and Rhoads took turns aft; Rodd remained at his radio. As busy as they had all been in the air, on the surface there seemed to be nothing for them to do. They rode along, swung high and low by the sea. The two engines sounded strangely soft, compared to the roar of four aloft.

At seven o'clock, just when the One and Three were landing at Halifax, they spotted a destroyer about ten miles to the north. Read directed Stone and Hinton to make for her, but she was moving too fast in the opposite direction, most certainly searching for them. Read finally signaled the pilots to resume the westerly course.

About seven-fifteen Rodd hurried forward to Read. "They made it, Commander," he said. "I just heard the message. They've landed at Halifax."

Read released a rare grin. "Good. That's fine. Tell the others."

When Breese heard the news he said to Smokey Rhoads, "You should have saved that bottle. We could use it now."

In a half-hour it was dark. The wind went down and the sea grew smooth and a big moon came up early. They were able to sustain a speed of ten knots. Read's only concern was for the remaining two engines; if they held up there would be nothing to worry about.

Around midnight Read decided the full crew need not stay on duty and he gave orders that Stone and Hinton could spell each other at the controls and that Breese and Rhoads could do likewise in the rear lookout. He also told Herbert Rodd to give up his radio watch. "On a clear night like this we'll probably see help long before we could hear it on that machine," he said. Read granted himself a few cat naps during the night.

He resigned himself to failure. Whether the fault was human or mechanical, here he was chugging across the Atlantic in the middle of the night, out of the air, out of the race, out of what might have been a share in the Navy's greatest moment in aviation. What would happen now? Somehow or other they would make shore; he'd turn the Four over to mechanics—or a junk buyer, perhaps—sign a paper that relieved him of the responsibility of her, then go back to Washington, back to a desk, and that would be it. His fellow officers would, he knew, simply say he was the victim of bad luck, but this would not erase his own hint of guilt. If only he had— Oh, well.

At dawn they saw the lights of a steamer, far ahead. They tried to head her off but she was going too fast and dropped beyond the horizon quickly. They resumed their western course. The strain of the sudden rush proved too much for the two engines: they coughed wearily several times, then died.

Breese said, "This is getting a little disgusting." Without awaiting instructions from Read, he wiggled his way through the superstructure and went to work. After ten minutes he got the starboard engine going, and the Four went around in huge circles for fifteen minutes while he inched across to the port engine to make repairs.

At five-twenty-five, they sighted the first lighthouse on Cape Cod, strangely lonely in the haze of morning. A few minutes later they passed the second lighthouse, and just as the sun's first warmth touched them they arrived off the Naval Air Station at Chatham. Read gave the signal to turn in.

They were still about two miles off shore when they saw two seaplanes take off from Chatham, obviously to search for them. The planes spotted them before rising more than five hundred feet, hurried over for a closer look, then circled triumphantly. The pilots waved down at the crew of the NC-4; the crew waved back at the pilots. The Four chugged awkwardly onward toward Chatham like a lame duck, nevertheless proud she had got home on her own. For a moment, Read's downhearted crew managed to rally their sagging spirits.

Then, less than a mile from shore, the two engines conked out again and the ship was helpless.

Jim Breese's shoulders slumped and he said, "I feel like an orphan."

V

THE BRITISH PILOTS at Saint Johns took the news soberly: two of the American seaplanes were already at Halifax, ready to continue on to Newfoundland as soon as the weather permitted. It was the weather that was holding back the British, and now apparently the weather was acting in favor of the Americans. The British scoffed at American claims that the Navy fliers were not involved in any air race and that they would not be permitted to accept the *Daily Mail* prize even if they qualified for it. There was more to be considered than the money; there was the honor, and the British were just as anxious to capture it as the fifty thousand dollars. Until the NCs One and Three landed at Halifax, there was every indication that, regardless of which team of British pilots made the transatlantic flight first, the triumph would be England's. But now the British confidence began to waver and the pilots were unnerved. The approaching Americans stirred a new and greater interest in the race. The names of Towers and Bellinger were heard in Newfoundland bars as often as those of Alcock and Brown, of Hawker and Grieve, of Cyril Porte, who had just arrived from England with his highly acclaimed Handley-Page. Overnight, the betting money switched to the Americans. Although they had still to arrive at Newfoundland for the big hop across the sea, the mere fact that they were en route by air gave their effort a dramatic impact that the Englishmen had lost because of their repeated delays. The rush of American reporters to Newfoundland added to the tension. The day before there had been scarcely a word about the flight in American papers; now, on Friday, May 9, front pages across the country bannered the new trinity of aviation heroes: Towers, Bellinger, Read. The weather-locked English pilots at Saint Johns found themselves villains in the competition to fly the Atlantic first. No matter what the Navy said, it was a race. And everybody knew it.

2

Early Friday morning a radioman abroad the *Baltimore* took a message to Towers's quarters. It was from Read at Chatham, and it said: "PROBABILITY GOOD ENGINE REPAIRS 48 HOURS. CAN YOU WAIT?" Before Towers could reply, instructions came from Washington: Don't wait. Towers therefore radioed Read: "NAVY DEPARTMENT ORDERS EARLIEST FLIGHT CONTINUATION. SORRY."

But Towers soon began having troubles of his own. The strain of the nine-hour flight from Rockaway had cracked the Olmstead propellers on both the One and Three. Towers inspected the damage after breakfast, then returned to the *Baltimore* to consult with his crews.

"We can't go on with cracked props," he said. "They could splinter in mid-air, and then we'd be in a mess."

Bellinger said, "Why didn't anybody think of shipping spares here as well as Newfoundland?"

Towers raised his arms helplessly. There was no excuse; it was just one of those oversights that could ruin everything.

"Well," said Richardson, "let's get some. Radio Glenn Curtiss to fly some up here right away."

"That's all we can do," Towers conceded.

Dick Byrd sat in a corner frowning. "Just a minute," he said. "I commanded our base here during the war and we had some Olmsteads then—I'm sure of it."

"Do you think they're still here?" Towers asked.

"I'm pretty sure they were here when I left, but what happened since I don't know."

"Check it out."

Byrd went ashore to hunt through warehouses of the Navy base and his heart sank when he was told that most of them were already empty.

Meanwhile Towers ordered his mechanics to remove the damaged propellers. "We'll have to sit here until we get some new ones from somewhere," he said. He noticed Barin's bandaged wrist. "What happened to you?"

Barin put his arm behind him. "It's nothing."

Bellinger spoke up. "It happened yesterday, Jack, while

we were tying up to a buoy here. The wind caught us and it looked as if we would crash into the buoy. Lou saw it and ran forward to hold the buoy off, and he slipped and hurt himself."

Towers asked, "Is your wrist broken?"

"No," Barin said. "Just sprained. I saw the doctor."

"Can you use it?" Towers asked.

Barin tried to end the discussion. "Sure. I'm okay."

Towers sank back in his chair. "Yeah, we're all okay," he said, a frown of despair heavy on his face. "We haven't got a thing in the world to worry about."

3

Putty Read was feeling equally glum. The two patrol planes that had spotted the Four outside the Chatham harbor circled over her for several moments, notifying the base that the search was over. Small craft came out to the fallen NC and towed her in. As soon as the crew stepped ashore, Read told Jim Breese, "Check her over thoroughly and let me know what has to be done."

While Breese worked, Read sent his messages to Towers, to Roosevelt and to Rockaway. The replies were so sympathetic that Read considered himself out of the trip before Breese could even report how badly off the plane was.

"The cracked engine is beyond repair," Breese said. "We'll have to get a replacement or we can't go on."

Read asked the Chatham base engineer, "Do you have a Liberty?"

"Yes, sir, but she's only a three-hundred horse."

"Can we use that as far as Halifax?" Read asked Breese.

"It'll have to be all the way to Trepassey," Breese said. "I don't think there's any spare equipment at Halifax."

Read said, "Well, can it get us to Trepassey?"

74

"We can try."

"Let's try. How long will it take you to install it?"

"That all depends," said Breese. "Rhoads and I will have to do the job ourselves. Maybe we can finish it today, most likely tomorrow sometime."

"Is Rhoads okay?" Read asked.

Breese shrugged. "He's all right now."

"Then get to work." Read turned to the other officers. "The rest of you might as well get some sleep. Rodd, see that the intercom is repaired, will you?"

"Yes, sir."

There was nothing to do now but wait. Quarters were provided for crew members who had no chores to perform. When Read awoke at two in the afternoon he went down to the beach to see how Breese was getting on. A cluster of Chatham personnel surrounded Breese, handing him tools as he worked.

"We should be out of here first thing in the morning," Breese said, almost cheerfully.

"Are you sure?" Read asked.

"Thanks to these guys," Breese said, indicating the Chatham mechanics with a nod of his head.

"That's fine," Read said. "I'll notify Command."

4

Late that afternoon, Towers was called to the *Baltimore*'s ship-to-shore telephone and recognized Byrd's excited voice. "I found the propellers, Jack," Byrd said. "A half-dozen of them."

"That's great," said Towers. "We need four."

"I know. Now you have extras in case you have more trouble."

"God forbid. How fast can you get them over here, Dick?"

"They're being loaded on a truck now. You should have them in an hour. When will you take off?"

Read's major concern was the two days of flying time that separated him from Towers. His low-power engine would be a serious obstacle, holding him back when he wanted to rush forward. He tried to brush from his mind the horrendous thoughts of what could happen to him as he limped his way north. Short of power, he might not even get away from Chatham, despite Breese's cautious optimism. On one visit to the Chatham radio room he learned of the propeller damages to the One and Three, and he allowed himself to take brief heart from the news. If the others were held up, he might be able to catch up with them. He sent a message to Towers, suggesting that they meet at Trepassey, but Towers replied that the Navy had ordered him to continue as quickly as possible. Now, with the new engine installed, Read sent another message, expressing his hopes for a take-off the next morning and that, depending on how the Four behaved, he might try to fly directly to Trepassey. His hopes were quickly shattered when the day's newspapers arrived and he saw a report from Washington that Roosevelt considered the Four out of the race.

Towers glanced at his watch. "I don't think today, Dick. By the time the props are installed it will be five or six o'clock. It's at least a six-hour flight to Trepassey, which would mean arriving at night and I don't want to try that. We can take off the first thing in the morning. I heard from Putty Read; he expects to take off from Chatham tomorrow and go straight through to Trepassey."

"That's a long haul for one day," Byrd pointed out.

"Even if he makes it in two days we should be ready to start out for the Azores on Monday—unless something else happens."

"I'm glad I remembered those propellers," Byrd said.

"So am I. You saved our lives."

Byrd laughed comfortably. "I've been miserable that I can't make this trip with you just because of that so-called overseas duty I did during the war right here at Halifax. But now I don't mind. Finding those propellers was worth it."

"It sure was," Towers said. "I'll have a drink for you when we get to the other side."

The remark was a whistle in the dark. Towers was well aware that he would need more than new propellers to get him to the other side of the Atlantic—for a drink or anything else. Already too much had gone wrong, and they hadn't even started yet. More than anything they needed a little of the factor over which they had no control: they needed a little luck. They tried to talk themselves into it. At Halifax, in an effort to escape the woes that haunted them, the two crews settled down to a session of poker, and when any of them drew into a straight or a flush the others all laughed and said they were glad to have such a lucky man along. In this way they eased a bit, and they were able to look forward to tomorrow with less apprehension. Tomorrow would be different; tomorrow would be better; tomorrow was going to be a great day.

Tomorrow dawned with full promise. The weather at Halifax and at Chatham was excellent. It was almost too beautiful a day to ruin in the rush of activity. In more dire circumstances, take-offs would have been scheduled for sunrise, but it was eight o'clock before the two crews at Halifax settled in their cockpits, the moorings were released and the order went out from Towers to start the engines. Aboard the One, Bellinger's engines responded immediately.

Aboard the Three, Towers barked into the intercom, "Richardson, I said start engines."

"I heard," Richardson responded. A muttering came over the phone, then Richardson said, "Something's wrong with the starters. Maybe they're cold."

Towers said, "Try again."

Richardson tried again. At last the hand starter on the two center engines coughed, sputtered, smoked, then caught.

"That's good," Towers encouraged.

But the outer engines remained lifeless. Richardson called: "Commander, it's the automatic starter. It won't turn over."

"Damn," Towers said.

Dick Byrd, in the forward cockpit with Towers, pointed out that the NC-1 was moving into take-off position. Towers contacted his radioman. "Lavender, give Pat Bellinger my instructions to take off. We'll catch up with him. Then ask the *Baltimore* to send over a new automatic starter; they ought to have one."

Cleared for take-off, Bellinger signaled for the NC-1 to turn into the wind. Her four engines roaring triumphantly, the One began to move ahead, passing the *Baltimore* and the Three just as she lifted from the water. The *Baltimore* blasted a good-luck on her horns and Towers waved at Bellinger as the One rose into the clear sky. The roar of the departing plane gave way to the guttural sputter of the speedboat from the *Baltimore* that came alongside. Machinist Mate L. R. Moore stretched from the Three's hull to take the automatic starter that was held out to him, then he ducked inside to make the repairs. In fifteen minutes he shouted to Richardson, "Try her now, Commander."

Richardson pushed the starter button on the panel in front of him. The stubborn outer engines kicked over at his touch.

"Pilot to Commander," Richardson announced on the intercom. "Ready for take-off."

"Let's go," Towers said.

The take-off was smooth and uneventful—almost a disappointment in view of the dramatic effect Towers had hoped to achieve in a twin take-off with the One. But now he consoled himself with the thought that it was still too early in the flight to fret about dramatic effects; there would be drama enough in the landing at the Azores. He watched as Byrd manipulated the navigation instruments and quickly brought the plane on course. Halifax fell away. In the clear morning air the rugged hills of Nova Scotia looked like a rumpled bear rug. To the north and to the east stretched the gray Atlantic, both inviting and forbidding. Somewhere up ahead was the One, waiting to be rejoined.

The Three rushed to make up for lost time. The distance to Trepassey was 460 miles—a seven-hour trip at the cruising speed the NCs had demonstrated. Towers tried to make himself comfortable for the long journey.

They had gone about forty miles when Towers heard what sounded like a rifle shot. Before Towers could turn around, he felt the plane take a sharp starboard dip and there was a distinct decrease in speed.

The machinist came in on the intercom. "Skipper, I think we lost the starboard prop."

Towers looked over at it and saw that the propeller was fluttering and rotating slower than the others. "Cracked?"

"Looks like it."

Towers called to McCulloch at the controls. "Dave, take her down." There was restrained disgust in his voice. "Moore, when we land go out and check the prop. If she's cracked we'll have to return to Halifax." Then to Byrd: "And I thought this was going to be such a beautiful day."

Dave McCulloch slid the Three to a gentle landing in the swells of the coast. Before the plane slowed to a stop, Moore, his emergency tool kit strapped like a belt to his waist, hoisted himself onto the hull, moved quickly to the wing structure, then out the starboard wing to the damaged propeller. He called above the wind, "Yes, she's out, Commander."

"Can we use her at all?" Towers shouted at him.

Moore shrugged and shook his head. "She's no good; she has to be replaced."

Towers studied his watch and cursed. It was fifteen minutes to ten, local time. Returning to Halifax meant the morning was a complete loss, but there was nothing else to do. "All right," Towers said. "Let's go back."

They were at Halifax at ten-thirty. Repairmen aboard the *Baltimore* had been forewarned by radio, and when the Three, flying low, limped back to her Halifax mooring a small boat of mechanics was already there, ready to help Moore install the new propeller. The job took over an hour. A message came from the *Baltimore:* would the Three's crew like to come aboard for lunch?

Towers replied, "No, thanks. Nobody gets out of this coffin this side of Trepassey."

They were able to take off again at twenty minutes to twelve, and this time they had no trouble. By now the NC-1 was far ahead of them; there was no chance of catching up and no reason to order the One to go slow enough to let them do so. In the midafternoon—at three-forty-one—Bellinger was over Trepassey Bay, awaiting landing instructions from the U.S.S. *Aroostock,* a supply ship sent ahead from

Boston. The *Aroostock* reported some low turbulence of unpredictable duration and asked Bellinger if he had enough fuel to remain aloft for a while until a weather improvement. Bellinger did. He circled the bay at 3,500 feet for half an hour. Then reports came from patrol ships, announcing the development of a bad storm that was probably producing winds up to forty-five miles an hour. It was a big storm, advancing along the East Coast, and nobody knew how long it would last. The *Aroostock* suggested that Bellinger had better attempt a landing and gave him full information of cross winds and surface action. Mitscher and Barin tensed at their controls, aware that they would have to make a landing at high speed in order to prevent the wind from keeling over their plane. They came in low and fast, hitting the water with an impact that made the whole plane shudder, then they bobbed quickly to the lee side of the *Aroostock* for safety.

Four hours later—at seven-thirty-one—Towers called in that he was over Trepassey. By now the gale winds had hit the bay, making a landing difficult and dangerous. Again the *Aroostock* radioed the question: "Can you wait a while?" Towers could. For almost an hour he circled the bay above the storm, watching the sun move farther west.

He called the *Aroostock:* "I don't want to come down in the pitch dark."

"It's still bad down there," came the reply. "Do you want to try it?"

"What's the forecast?"

"No improvement."

"What about Saint Johns?"

"Socked in."

"Well, there's no place else to go. I'm coming in."

The Three dropped a thousand feet into the clouds and

began to shake fiercely. On the intercom Towers announced: "Pilots, it's up to you. Everybody else hold on." To Byrd: "Let's get out of here."

They left the forward cockpit, worked their way around the fuel tanks in the middle of the plane and went aft to the radio compartment. They descended another thousand feet. Towers told Lavender, "Tell them to let us know when they see us."

The *Aroostock* replied: "We hear you but we can't see you."

Another thousand feet down.

Then the message: "There you are. You're doing fine. Hold your decline. Your path is clear. What's your speed?"

Lavender answered: "Sixty-five."

"Decrease to fifty when you have a hundred-foot altitude. Small craft are standing by to escort you the rest of the way in case you have to ditch."

Lavender gave the instructions to Richardson and McCulloch. Towers went to the center cockpit and thrust his head up between the two pilots. "Okay?"

"It's a mess," McCulloch said.

"Can you see anything?"

Richardson said, "Just about."

"What's the altitude?"

"Two-fifty," said McCulloch.

"Two hundred," Richardson corrected immediately.

"You've got your instructions," Towers reminded.

McCulloch said, "I see the escort."

"Take her in," Towers said.

The sudden dip and loss of speed knocked Towers off balance. He grabbed at the pilot's bench to brace himself. He gripped tensely, his eyes absently on McCulloch's knees.

"Hold tight," Richardson said softly.

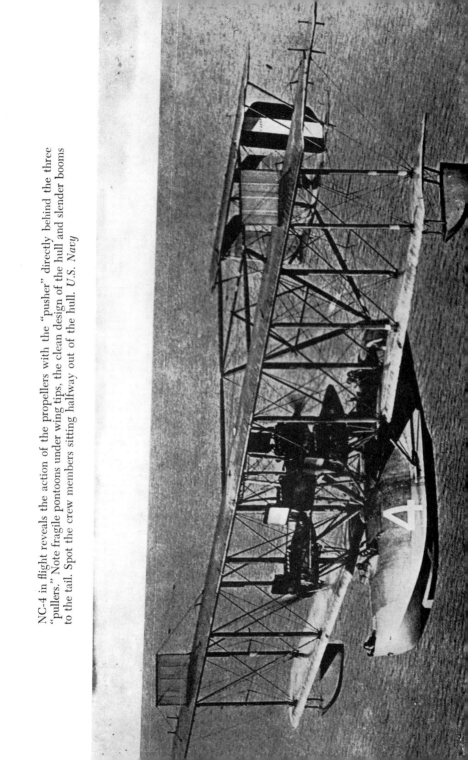

NC-4 in flight reveals the action of the propellers with the three "pullers." Note fragile pontoons under wing tips, the clean design of the hull and slender booms to the tail. Spot the crew members sitting halfway out of the hull. *U.S. Navy*

Above, close-up of the engines. *U.S. Navy.* Above right, the pilot's cramped cockpit, simple compass and tiny windscreen. Right, Lt. Cmdr. Richard Byrd tests his drift-indicator for Lt. Cmdr. "Putty" Read. *F. Ryberg, N. Y. World*

The three NC crews stand at attention in front of the hangar at Rockaway Beach, Long Island, as Commander Towers, the C.O. of the flight, reads the official orders commissioning squadron to make trip. *U.S. Navy*

April 28, 1919, the crew of the NC-1 pose for photo. Left to right: Lt. Cmdr. Bellinger, Lt. Cmdr. Mitscher, Lt. Barin, Lt. Sadenwater, Chief Machinist's Mate Kesler and Engineer Christensen. *United Press International*

April 19, 1919, the NC-3 crew in front of their plane. Left to right: Cmdr. Towers, Cmdr. Richardson, Lt. McCulloch, Lt. Cmdr. Lavender, Engineer Moore and Lt. Rhodes. The last was left at Trepassey. *United Press International*

Crew of the NC-4, the "Jinx" plane, posed at Rockaway prior to flight. Left to right: Lt. Cmdr. Read, Lt. Stone, Lt. Hinton, Ensign Rodd, Chief Machinist Howard (who was injured by a prop and replaced by Chief Machinist's Mate Rhoads) and Lt. Breese. *International News Photos*

Lt. C. E. Ruttan was one of two Navy artists assigned to the NC project. He observed planes and crews, watched them prepare and then take off on the actual flight. Two of his paintings are: above, a destroyer lighting the way for the NC-4, below, NC-3 down at sea. *U.S. Navy*

The successful crew of the NC-4, still in their leatherette flying suits, are shown aboard a U.S. Navy ship wearing happy smiles. At right are Towers, Bellinger plus Navy brass who met them. *Topical Press Agency*

Left, unusual shot of the NC-4 occurred when plane landed in Lisbon at dusk. Waiting photogs complained, so next day at dawn, Read and crew took up plane, circled city and landed for movies. *United Press International.* Right, the two surviving members of the NC-4, Eugene Rhoads and Putty Read, on a trip in 1949 commemorating their historic flight. *Wide World Photos*

Crew of the NC-4 are given
parade through the streets
Plymouth, England. The Briti
gave the Navy pilots a wild n
ception. Prince of Wales an
Winston Churchill embrace
them. *U.S. Navy*

The loser and winner of r
transatlantic air race sha
hands. Harry Hawker, probal
greatest pilot of his day, crash
in the Atlantic trying to b
Read. In the nip-and-tuck ra
Hawker's luck ran out. *Uni
Press International*

Back home, the NC crews
were met on the steps of the
Navy Department building
by the Secretary of the Navy,
Josephius Daniels, and Asst.
Secretary Franklin Delano
Roosevelt. *U.S. Navy*

The New York Times.

III. NO. 22,494

NEW YORK, WEDNESDAY, MAY 28, 1919, THIRTY-TWO PAGES.

THE WEATHER

Fair Wednesday and probably Thursday; gentle variable winds.

TWO CENTS

-4 WINS FIRST OCEAN FLIGHT FOR AMERICA; HOURS FROM PONTA DELGADA TO LISBON; AWKER'S PLANE PICKED UP BY AMERICAN SHIP

REDS
LSHEVIKI
TROGRAD

, and Finns in
ty After Se-
of Fighting.

GERMANY DEMANDS

British and U. S. Marines
Land at Danzig from Big Fleet

PARIS, May 27 (Havas.)—
British and American Marines
have been landed at the Baltic
Port of Danzig, according to a
dispatch received here from War-
saw.

A powerful fleet, it is added,
will be anchored off the harbor
there.

AZORES
LISBON
PORTUGAL

Route of the NC-4 From Ponta Delgada to Lisbon.

LEAVES THE AZORES 6:18 A. M., OUR TIME

Arrives at Portuguese Port at 4:02
P. M., Averaging Over 82
Miles an Hour.

START FOR PLYMOUTH TODAY WITH GOOD WEATHER

WEATHER

day

s Life.
and Discontent.
y. 2 Japanese.

BRISBANE.

S WEATHER

TWO

The Washington Times EXTRA

NUMBER 11,177. WASHINGTON, TUESDAY EVENING, MAY 27, 1919. PRICE TWO CENTS

NC-4 REACHES LISBON

ORK HERALD.

WEDNESDAY, MAY 28, 1919.   PRICE TWO CENTS

A POWERFUL FACT.

S. AIRM O CROSS ATLANTIC; NC-4 REA N IN RECORD FLIGHT; ACTUA A FLYING TIME 26 HOURS

.S' STRIKE P D—RAH! RAH! READ

Mirror

R DAILY PICTURE PAPER

[16 PAGES.]   One Penny.

LONDON STREETS

After epic flight, Albert C. Read became just another Navy officer. Left, he is shown rear admiral, last rank before retiring. He'd gladly make trip all over again. Patri Bellinger (center) reached rank of vice admiral before leaving Navy. During World W II when the NC-4 was being scrapped he saved it for the Smithsonian Institution. In t struggle between ship officers and flying officers, the Navy passed John Towers (righ over in rank. FDR personally promoted him, and he became one of the best strateg admirals of World War II. *U.S. Navy photos*

Far left, Mitsch as a vice admiral. I became pilot of t NC-1 after his NC was scrapped, we on to become a gre hero of air combat Pacific. Navy Secr tary Forrestal wc shiped Mitscher. *U. Navy.* Aide, Arleiy Burke, left, nc heads Navy. *Culv Pictures, Inc.*

Vice Admiral Richard E. Byrd (left) departed Navy after trapeze tumble left him wi limp. World War I brought him back. His inventions made flight possible. Later he fl to North and South Poles, won Medal of Honor. *U.S. Navy.* Nicest man in the Navy a on the NC flight was Holden Richardson (right). The "old" man of the flight was brilliant designer; his hull is still model for all seaplanes. He was captain, ret., at dea

The plane hit a rising wave and groaned in pain. Water flooded over Towers. Instinctively he glanced down to see if the hull had split and when he saw the inch of water sloshing at his feet his eyes widened in terror. But then he looked up and saw that Richardson and McCulloch were drenched and he realized the water had come in through the open cockpits. The heaving motion of the plane increased as it slowed down. The two pilots gave their attention to the boats that guided them to the *Aroostock*. Relieved, Towers left the cockpit and returned to the radio compartment, where he gave Dick Byrd an appraising look that seemed to ask just how bad things were going to get before they started getting better.

Byrd was scheduled to go only as far as Trepassey. He said to Towers, "End of the line."

Towers said, "I wish to hell it were."

5

At Chatham, Putty Read was beginning to suspect he had already reached the end of his line. As at Halifax, his day got off to a fine start. The weather was good. Breese and Smokey Rhoads were at work on the new engine early, and by ten o'clock they were ready for tests. Rhoads stood on the wing, his gaze lovingly upon the new engine; Breese climbed into the pilot's cockpit. He pressed the automatic-starter button. Nothing happened. He pressed it again.

"Smokey," he called, "check your sparks. I'm not getting anything out of the starter."

Rhoads made a quick inspection. "Everything looks all right here."

Breese tried the starter button again. Nothing. "Now what?" he said. He crawled under the panel board and checked the connections but could find nothing wrong.

Then he went out for a look at the starter itself. "Here's the trouble," he said to Rhoads. "It's on the fritz."

"Can it be fixed?" Rhoads asked.

"I doubt it. Let's find Read."

Read was not too disturbed. "Ask the base engineer for another one. They ought to have some here."

But they did not—at least not the right kind. Read said, "Then we're stuck here until we can get one. Radio Rockaway and find out how long it will take to fly a starter up here."

Rockaway had a suggestion that could save time: a plane would leave immediately for Montauk with a starter; send a faster plane from Chatham to pick it up there. The commander of the Chatham base immediately ordered one of his pilots to take off for Montauk in a small, fast seaplane, but as the pilot taxied into the open water he struck a sandbar, nosed over and broke his propeller. The commander decided to send the base blimp after the starter; it would be slower but surer. By the time the blimp got into the air and disappeared toward the southern horizon a message came from Montauk: the Rockaway plane was there and was willing to continue on to Chatham if Read wished.

"Fine," Read said. "Tell him to come on."

It was late afternoon before the starter arrived, was installed and put to work. Read was restless and eager to get going. The flight to Halifax would take him six hours, bringing him in after dark, but he was willing to try it. He knew, however, that the original flight plans banned any night landings, so he decided it would be wise for him to get approval before leaving Chatham. He sent a radio query to Trepassey, where he expected the two sister ships to be, and he was surprised to learn that Towers was still two hours out. At the same time, he received weather reports from both Trepassey and Washington that the sudden storm off Newfoundland now looked likely to blanket the entire route north from Chatham, and he was ordered to remain at Cape Cod until the gale passed.

"That settles it," Read told his crew. "We'll have to spend the night here, but I want us airborne tomorrow at dawn. If everything works right we should be at Trepassey tomorrow night."

But the next night they were still at Chatham. And they were there Monday night and Tuesday night, landlocked by the raging storm. Read's only consolation was knowing that Towers and Bellinger were similarly grounded at Trepassey by the same storm. His unrest, on the other hand, was in knowing that the storm would probably clear at Newfoundland before it did at Cape Cod and that his fellow commanders were apt to take off without giving him a chance to catch up with them. He was aware that there would be no malice in their decision to go ahead without him; there were too many uncertainties involved in the flight to change plans or miss opportunities for the sake of friendship or loyalty. Whoever could make the flight should make it, and that was all that mattered.

Early on the morning of Wednesday, May 14, in the process of rolling over in his sleep, Read awakened and, from habit, listened for the wind outside. The morning seemed calm. He looked at his watch; it was shortly after five. Prepared for disappointment, he got up from bed and walked across to a window and raised the shade. In the predawn darkness he could see only the silhouettes of things. He studied a tree for a moment; there was little movement in its bare branches. He pulled the window up full, leaned out and sniffed the air. The heavy moisture had gone out of it; compared to the past three days, the wind that touched his cheek was Arizona-dry.

He turned back to the room and clicked on a lamp and

looked at the clock again. Five-fifteen. Quickly he donned his trousers and went down the hall of the Visiting Officers Quarters to the room shared by the pilots. He tapped lightly. The door was opened almost immediately by Hinton, his face hidden by shaving cream.

"The storm has passed," Read said.

"Yes, I know," Hinton said. "I was just going to wake you."

"Is Stone up?"

"Yes, sir."

"Get ready as soon as you can. I'll wake the others."

"I've already telephoned Breese and Rodd," Hinton said, "and I sent a runner to wake up Smokey."

"Good," said Read. "I'll see you at the plane in fifteen minutes."

On Sunday, because of the high winds, the NC-4 had been towed ashore and placed in a hangar. On Monday and Tuesday, for the lack of anything else to do, the crew had loafed in her shadow, guarding her by silent agreement against the gremlins that seemed to haunt her. Her tanks were full, her engines were oiled, her cabin was as clean and orderly as a new bride's house.

As Read reached the hangar, Breese and Smokey Rhoads were cautiously guiding a Chatham mechanic at the wheel of a tow. Moving outdoors, the Four greeted the first streaks of the clear morning with what struck Breese as the nervous joy of a colt.

Read called, "All okay?"

"Shipshape," Breese replied.

"You men have breakfast?"

"It's being cooked now. We're a little early."

"Where are the others?"

Breese pointed. "In the weather shack."

Read went to join the pilots.

"It's a beautiful day," Hinton greeted him.

"Let's hope so," said Read, wary of too much enthusiasm. "What about Trepassey?"

"Should be clearing this morning, according to the oh-five-hundred report. It's a south wind; we got it first."

"Let's take advantage of it," Read said. "As soon as you've finished here go have your breakfast. I want to be out of here in a half-hour."

At the radio shack, Read notified Trepassey, Halifax, Rockaway and Washington of his intentions to take off at six-thirty. He also asked the patrol ships between Chatham and Halifax to be on the lookout for him. Depending on the weather and the behavior of his plane, he added, he would either continue on to Trepassey after a brief stop at Halifax or perhaps try to make it through to Newfoundland in one hop. He also queried Towers about flight plans for the two planes with him. Towers replied that he expected clear weather by late afternoon. If reports across the Atlantic were encouraging he and Bellinger might attempt an early evening departure for the Azores, with expected arrival sometime Thursday afternoon.

Read radioed immediately: "IN EVENT YOUR DEPARTURE THIS AFTERNOON, REQUEST PERMISSION TO JOIN YOU AT SEA OFF HALIFAX."

Towers answered: "UNABLE DECIDE YOUR REQUEST AT THIS TIME. KEEP IN TOUCH."

A few minutes after seven, the NC-4 rolled down the Chatham seaplane ramp into the calm sea. Remembering what had happened to the plane that hit a sand bar on Saturday, Read requested a small-craft escort out to open water. In ten minutes, the Four was well clear of obstacles. On signal from Read, Hinton and Stone revved the engines to full speed, then relaxed them. They were ready now, after a week's delay.

Read said into the intercom, "Take-off." Then he lowered himself inside his navigator's cockpit to escape the rush of wind.

The plane performed beautifully. In a half-hour they were at three thousand feet, roaring north at ninety miles an hour. At one point, a strong tailwind pushed them forward to 109 miles an hour, faster than anyone had expected the NCs to go. The crew was confident and happy with each other. Even when, two hours out, the new engine began to sputter, Breese came consolingly on the intercom: "Don't worry about it, Commander. That always happens with a new engine. She'll clear."

Three hours out, a message was received: "WHAT IS YOUR POSITION? ALL KEENLY INTERESTED IN YOUR PROGRESS. GOOD LUCK. ROOSEVELT."

Read replied: "ROOSEVELT, WASHINGTON. THANK YOU FOR GOOD WISHES. NC-4 IS TWENTY MILES SOUTHWEST OF SEAL IS-LAND MAKING EIGHTY-FIVE MILES AN HOUR."

Back from Washington came: "ENTIRE EXCHANGE OF MES-SAGES ACHIEVED IN THREE MINUTES—ANOTHER NC TRIUMPH. CONGRATULATIONS. ROOSEVELT."

The NC-4 itself seemed to smile with pride.

Breese went to Radioman Rodd and said, "How about sending a message to my wife in New York?"

"I can't," Rodd said.

"Why not?"

"I just tried to send a message to my girl," Rodd said, "but the Marconi man in Maine who picked it up said he couldn't accept it."

"Why not?"

"He said his company had no rates listed for messages

from airplanes so he wouldn't know what to charge me."

"I'll be darned," said Breese, and they both laughed at what, at this glorious moment, struck them as the extreme stupidity of the groundhogs somewhere below them.

The NC-4 landed at Halifax three hours and fifty-one minutes after leaving Chatham, a record in speed for the awkward aircraft that were fast becoming the miracle of aviation. On boarding the *Baltimore,* Read radioed Towers that he expected to take off for Trepassey in a few minutes. Towers replied with congratulations, adding that the weather at Newfoundland was continuing to improve and that most likely the One and Three would leave for the Azores early the next morning. "Hope you are with us," he said.

This time it was Rhoads who brought the bad news. "It's the new engine, Commander," he reported sadly. "She's filthy. I expected her to take on some foreign matter, but I've just checked her and she's loaded. I'm going to have to clean her out."

"How long will that take?"

"A couple of hours."

"Is it really necessary?"

"I think so, sir, unless you want us to row our way to Newfoundland. I really ought to clean out all the engines."

"And how long would that take?"

"A good job would take a couple of days."

Read bit his lip. "Just clean the new engine. We'll take our chances with the others."

An hour passed and Smokey Rhoads was nowhere near the end of his job. Although it was only early afternoon, Read faced the fact that there was little hope he would be able to resume the flight to Trepassey in time to arrive before sunset. Forlorn, he sent the news to Towers. He got no reply, which unsettled him at first, but then the thought occurred to him that maybe Towers himself was suffering fresh woes. As sincerely as he struggled to put the negative idea out of his mind, he was still considering it as he fell asleep that night on the *Baltimore*. It gave him faint consolation against the horror of awakening in the morning to the news that Towers and Bellinger were en route to the Azores.

In the morning he did not ask for any news but weather reports. By nine o'clock, Rhoads declared that he had done everything on the new engine that could be achieved in the limited time allotted to him. Read gave the order for the crew members to take their stations. The bellowed farewell from the *Baltimore*'s horns reflected the tension at Halifax. This, Read knew, was his last chance to catch the sister ships. The NC-4 hurried out of Halifax Bay without pausing for a salute to the *Baltimore* crew, who had, in the past twenty hours, given her a name she quite plainly resented: The Lame Duck.

She seemed doomed by her new name. Eighteen miles out of Halifax the oil pressure on the center engine dropped severely. Elmer Stone brought the plane down in the smooth waters off the coast, and Breese and Rhoads scurried out on the wings to find out what had gone wrong. This time Rhoads refused to be rushed. Working carefully, he found that a piece of rubber had clogged one of the gas leaders to the motor and he removed it. He also insisted on cleaning the carburetor jets on all four engines and putting in a new spark plug for a cylinder that was refusing to fire. The job took him two hours, and when, at a quarter to one, he indicated to Read that the plane was ready he muttered, distinctly enough for Read to hear, "If I'd had time to do the job right in Halifax we wouldn't be bobbing around out here in the middle of the ocean."

There was no question now that he had done the job right this time. The four engines cooed like pigeons. The plane was speedily aloft, and Rhoads took his seat in the rear cockpit with blatant confidence, as if he knew none of the engines would dare falter for the rest of the trip.

Again a tailwind gave them extra thrust. On the 170-mile run from Cape Breton Island to Saint Pierre off Newfoundland they maintained a speed of over ninety-five knots. With a regularity that was comforting they passed over the patrol ships along their route, exchanging greetings in a holiday spirit. After Saint Pierre, Read took a quick and accurate reading, then gave Stone and Hinton the new course that would take them directly to Trepassey Bay. At three thousand feet, the ride was smooth, but it was cold. Ice formed on the struts. Whenever Read leaned out to check the drift indicator he felt as if he had poked his head into an Arctic wind tunnel.

About two hours out of Trepassey, Jim Breese was sitting in the rear cockpit, with no special task to occupy himself or his mind. He let his gaze rest on the sea below. Suddenly he saw a strange object and leaned across to Rhoads. "What's that thing?" he asked, and he pointed down.

Rhoads looked. The sight surprised him. "It's a dirigible," he said incredulously.

"What's it doing there?"

Rhoads shrugged. "I don't know. I didn't know there were any dirigibles up here."

Breese leaned over the side for a better view. "Looks like it's going backward."

"Maybe because we're going forward so fast," Rhoads suggested.

Read had seen the dirigible, too. Puzzled by it, he examined it with his binoculars. It was the C-5, a Navy craft, and it appeared to be out of control. Not only was it moving backward, but it wobbled and rolled wildly.

Read called Rodd on the intercom. "Find out what you can about a dirigible, the C-5, that seems to be in distress."

In a few moments, Rodd reported, "The dirigible is adrift. Broke from her moorings at Trepassey. We're told to ignore it."

Read made a note about the dirigible in his log, then returned his attention to the distance that still separated him from Trepassey.

Rodd picked up a message from Towers to Washington and gave it to Read: "WEATHER FAVORABLE. PREPARING FOR IMMEDIATE TAKE-OFF."

Read frowned at the message. Why couldn't they wait for him? He went into the hull to the pilot's cockpit and shouted up at Stone, "Elmer, can't you get more life out of this thing?"

"She's wide-open now," Stone said.

"Give her hell," Read ordered. Passing Rodd, he said, "Send our position to Trepassey. And let me have every word you get about their take-off."

Back in his own cockpit, Read found himself pressing against the hull, as if he could push more speed into the plane. He took a reading and estimated his position an hour out of Trepassey. Rodd reported, "The crews are entering their planes."

Infuriated, Read slammed his fist against the hull. "Come on, come on!"

A half-hour later, Rodd said, "The planes are taxiing into position for take-off."

Read said, "Send this message to Trepassey immediately: 'COMING IN FOR A LANDING.'"

"But we're fifty miles out of Trepassey," Rodd said.

"Send that message!" Read barked.

The message went out.

Despite the cold and wind, Read leaned out of his cockpit and strained his eyes for a hint of Cape Pine, the last landmark before Trepassey Bay, and when it finally popped above the horizon he instructed his pilots to descend to five hundred feet but to hold their speed. Suddenly there it was, almost close enough to touch, the bay, sparkling in the afternoon sun.

As the Four roared up the bay toward the *Aroostock* anchored at the inland end, Read saw the One and the Three taxiing at full speed at him.

"Wait! Wait!" Read hollered into the wind.

Impossible though it was, they seemed to have heard him. They slowed down and turned back to the *Aroostock*. Approaching at good speed, the Four was abreast of them as they nosed into their moorings. Motorboats came out from the *Aroostock* to pick up the three crews; Read was the last commander to climb the supply ship's ladder and salute the ensign. He turned quickly to Towers and saluted him, then offered his hand.

"Thanks a lot for waiting for us," Read said. "You almost got away."

Towers's face was a tornado of anger. "We weren't waiting for you, Putty," he said. "We've been trying since dawn to take off. But something's wrong. We can't get these coffins into the air."

"Oh," said Read quietly. "Sorry to hear that." And he smiled.

VI

"THE REAL MISERY," Towers said when they were over coffee in the *Aroostock's* wardroom, "has been those Englishmen. They've been hanging around here every day, laughing at us."

Bellinger said, "You can imagine what fun they've had the past couple of days, watching us waddle around the bay like pregnant ducks."

"Well, what's wrong?" Breese asked. "How come you can't take off?"

"It's weight," said Towers. "It must be weight, but we can't figure out which weight. We don't know what to throw away. Pat can get up a few feet, but he can't stay there, and the Three won't lift at all."

Read asked, "Did you have any trouble at Halifax?"

"None at all."

"What about your fuel tanks?" Read asked.

"They're full, of course," Towers said.

"Were they full at Halifax?"

"Not completely. They didn't have to be for this short trip, but they were full at Rockaway and we got off there without any trouble."

Read turned to Jim Breese. "Fuel consumption was your job. Got any idea what's happening?"

They all saw the growing smile on Breese's face and wondered why it was there.

"Maybe," Breese said. "When you filled up here, were you on land or in the water?"

"In the water," Towers said.

Now Breese's smile was a big grin. "That's it, then. On land the hull is level, so sixteen hundred gallons of gas comes right up to the 'full' mark I made on the glass gauge tube, but in the water the hull tilts forward so a full tank would be about an inch below the mark."

Towers grimaced. "In other words, we're carrying a couple of hundred extra pounds of gas?"

"About that."

"Did you know this would happen?"

"I knew that it could."

"Then why didn't you say something?"

"I didn't expect it to be a problem—as long as I was around to check out everybody's tanks," said Breese. "Now I'm glad I kept my mouth shut."

Understanding, Towers lost his anger. "We're just lucky we've had bad weather here or those Englishmen would be over on the other side by now, giving us the big horse laugh."

"Maybe we'll be laughing at them, now," Breese said.

Richardson put in, "Harry Hawker was telling me yesterday that at least three of the British planes would take off together as soon as they had good weather reports for the North Atlantic."

"We've got our good weather," Towers said confidently. He explained to Read, "The station ships have been reporting clear weather all the way to the Azores and they expect it to hold for a few days. How soon can you be ready?"

"A few hours," Read said. "We have to replace one engine, and the others need checking."

Byrd asked, "What about your propellers?"

"No trouble at all." Read turned to Towers. "I hear you had trouble with yours."

"Yes. It's the only thing that worries me. But they seem to be all right now. Pat, do you think you can be ready in the morning?"

Bellinger nodded. "Now that we know why we couldn't take off today, the One will be ready as soon as we drain off some of the fuel."

Read asked, "What happened to that dirigible we saw adrift?"

There was disappointment in Byrd's soft laugh. "That was my ticket to the Azores," he said. Interested, Read gave Byrd an inquiring look. Byrd explained, "It appears that the Navy wasn't taking any chances. At the last minute, the C-5 was ordered up here to make a flight to the Azores in case the NCs couldn't make it for any reason."

"That's strange," Read commented.

"Well," said Byrd, "I suppose the Navy felt that all those station ships were already strung out across the sea and they might as well be put to some use."

"But she broke loose?"

"Yes. Fortunately, the crew was ashore. When she broke, they tried to hold her in by the guide ropes, but the wind was too strong."

"Anybody hurt?" Read asked.

"One man was lifted twenty-five feet into the air by the ropes before he let go, but he wasn't hurt."

Read asked, "How did you figure into all this?"

Byrd grimaced wryly. "I was supposed to command the dirigible if she made the trip to the Azores."

Read understood Byrd's disappointment, but he also thought the dirigible plans were rather premature. "Well," he said, "then I guess it's up to the NCs to make the trip."

"The NCs or the English," Byrd said dismally.

The crews spent the rest of the afternoon at their planes, checking and rechecking every moving part. Satisfied, they went ashore in the evening to visit with the British pilots who had come over from Saint Johns. There was a great deal of boasting from both sides, plus generous ridicule by the British, who had not stopped laughing over the failure of the One and Three to take off. Reporters refused to accept Towers's insistence that the Americans were not engaged in any air race; they could not believe that the Navy fliers would decline the prize money if they qualified for it.

"Our only remuneration," Towers emphasized, "will be our regular Navy pay—and if we don't succeed we might not get even that."

Harry Hawker teased, "Why not be smart, Jack, and just sail across? Your planes look like they might be able to make it that way."

They all laughed, the Americans rather uncomfortably. "I'll give it some thought," Towers said, "and even that way we'll beat you to England."

By ten o'clock they were back aboard the *Aroostock*, where

Towers called a conference of his navigators and pilots. The session was held behind closed doors, and at it Towers revealed his revised flight plan. The destination—the Azores—was a cluster of small islands approximately thirteen hundred miles away. Arriving at them even in broad daylight in clear weather required navigation mastery; it would be wise to take no chances.

"So," Towers said, "we will leave here as late in the day as we can, which means we'll be making most of the distance at night. That will put us well toward the Azores at daybreak. If any of us has gone off course we shouldn't have too much trouble locating ourselves in the clear weather that's forecast. Our goal—" he turned to a map—"is Ponta Delgada, the capital. Navy personnel are already there, waiting for us. If you have any trouble—fuel shortage, props, engines, anything—make for Horta, two hundred miles west." He pointed to the island. Then he said, "Now, let's try to stick together so that we can make a good showing when we land. If for any reason we have to break formation you will get the orders from me. Keep in touch with me on your long-range radios, and if they go out contact me through the station ships along the route; that's why they're there." He sent an inquiring look around the room. "Any questions?"

No one spoke.

"Okay," he said, "let's get on to the next matter of business." He sat down at the conference table, extracted his wallet and placed it in front of him. "Let's get back to the poker game."

2

Friday morning, May 16, was cold and clear. The wind had changed, coming now from the north, and it promised a helpful push to the NCs on their southeasterly course. Work remained to be done on the Four; Jim Breese and Smokey Rhoads were at it early, confidently. By noon they were ready for tests. Trouble struck immediately when the new engine flooded. They drained it and dried it with the care they would give a baby, then tried again. The engine coughed, sputtered and spat, then broke into an impatient roar. They watched it warily. Breese muttered: "Come on, baby!" Responding, the engine subdued to a steady purr.

Similar tests were made by the sister ships, each taking turns taxiing in the quiet waters. On shore crowds gathered to watch. The British pilots, their North Atlantic path blocked by storms off Ireland, returned from Saint Johns to witness what they hoped would be another fiasco.

At one o'clock, the Americans went aboard the *Aroostock* for lunch. They were all too nervous to eat, but they tried to hide their apprehensions by eating too much.

Towers announced, "I estimate take-off at five o'clock. So we'd all better relax this afternoon, especially the pilots. Get some sleep."

Sleep was out of the question. The men loafed on the deck of the *Aroostock*, gazing out at their planes at mooring, or they wrote letters in which they could think of nothing to say. Towers, Bellinger and Read spent some of the time with Dick Byrd, practicing on the navigation instruments he had invented.

Byrd said, "The answer to your problem is to take me along."

Towers smiled sadly. "You know the rules, Dick."

"Unfortunately."

At four o'clock, the *Aroostock* cooks sent up word that they had prepared fresh sandwiches and coffee; should they take the food out to the planes? Towers said no. Grateful though he was for the thoughtfulness, he did not want strangers aboard the ships who, in their normal quest for souvenirs, might do damage. He said that the food should be given to the machinist mates.

Back came a query from C. I. Kesler, machinist for the One: "Now?"

"When we board," Towers replied.

By four-thirty, the *Aroostock* had the tension of an opening night. Small boats were brought alongside to take the NC crews to their planes. All *Aroostock* crewmen not on specific duty were permitted on deck to watch. The crowd ashore was now a record for Trepassey. Motorboats, forewarned to remain outside the take-off path, darted like water beetles in the distance.

At a quarter to five, Towers came from the wardroom, leading Bellinger and Read. Their crews saw them and fell in behind their skippers automatically. Officers of the *Aroostock* were gathered at the ladder that dropped to the waiting boats. The fliers approached them in a reluctant group, like a street gang unsure of itself. When finally Towers spoke to the ship's officers his voice was strangely hushed. He thanked them for their hospitality and all their help and, in an effort at a joke, he said he guessed they would be glad to get rid of his men at last. In reply, the captain of the *Aroostock* said that, on the contrary, he had been glad to have them all aboard, he wished he could be at the other end of the trip to welcome them in their victory, and he wished them luck.

Then Towers turned to his men. "We'll take off in the same formation as Rockaway. I'll lead, you to port, Putty, and you at starboard, Pat."

Bellinger said, "Aye, aye, sir." And was immediately embarrassed by his impulsive formality.

100

Read nodded.

Towers turned and saluted the ship's ensign, then took the salute from the Officer of the Day. In a moment he was quickly making his way down the ladder to the waiting motorboats. Then Bellinger and his crew went through the process, then Read with his men. In a matter of minutes they were all in the boats, ready to move out to the planes. Towers gave the signal and the boats roared away. The *Aroostock* personnel lined the railing, watching. Ashore, crowds moved closer to the water.

Read was uneasy. He said to Jim Breese, "I wish we could have waited another day. This is a long hop to make with engines we haven't even tested yet."

Breese shrugged. "Everything will be all right, Skipper."

"I hope so," Read said softly.

The boats nosed close to the planes. The men went aboard and took their places with impatient familiarity. The orders came from Towers: "Warm up engines." On shore, the crowds saw the puffs of smoke as the engines coughed to life. Excitement grew with a rising murmur.

There was trouble on the Four. The new engine would not turn over. Jim Breese looked up at it and cursed. New engines were always coated with an oil preservative to prevent rust and which was supposed to burn up when the engine was started, but sometimes the oil clogged and caused the engine to cut off. Each time, this required cleaning twenty-four spark plugs and replacing them, a long and tedious chore. In testing the engine, Breese and Rhoads had cleaned the plugs three times before they were satisfied. And now the engine was acting up again.

"I'm going to soup up the thing," Breese told Rhoads.

The engine had an eight-volt ignition system. In the hull, Breese had a stand-by twelve-volt battery. Breese pushed the battery into position and said to Rhoads, "Tell the pilots to push the starter button when I say so." Then he took out his pocket knife and opened the blades into a square U. "Now," Breese said. The pilots pushed the button. Using the knife as a contact, Breese connected the battery to the ignition system. The engine gave out a loud bark, like a pistol shot, then sputtered to life. When Breese removed the knife, he saw that his hand was badly burned. "Well, at least the crazy thing is running," he said.

Towers ordered, "Report."

Bellinger answered, "All set."

From Read came "Ready for take-off."

"Take positions," Towers instructed.

There was a great roar as the three planes moved away from the *Aroostock* and glided smoothly to clear water. Small craft along the shore puttered eastward to stay abreast of the planes.

From the Three, Lavender radioed Towers's vital message: "Take-off in one minute."

The order sent tremors through every man and brought nervous smiles to anxious faces. Read tried to make himself comfortable in his forward cockpit. Bellinger looked over at him and nodded, his encouraging grin too weak to travel the distance between them. The pilots of the Four and One watched the Three ahead of them, alert for a forward movement. Breese gave his new engines a final glance of hope.

The Three began to move. Seeing it, the *Aroostock* opened all her horns. Ashore, the crowds began to jump and wave and scream, and the small craft shot forward as eager as bees.

The long clear bay before them, the three planes lumbered into the thirty-mile wind that blew in from the sea. Heavy and deep in the water, they moved slowly at first, gulping at the wind. As the Four picked up speed, she inched ahead of the One at her right and closed the space to the Three. This was no time to worry about appearances; Putty Read gave his pilots the signal to ignore the formation and keep going.

In the hull, Jim Breese studied his watch. He knew how long it should take to get up and he could see that the Four was dragging. He realized that the Four, too, was undoubtedly having weight problems. He had taken aboard two cans of lubricating oil, each weighing thirty-five pounds. He looked at them and said, "I'll want that oil if we're ever forced down! But if we never take off I won't need it." He grabbed the cans and threw them overboard. The Four responded with a slight lift, and as she was leaving the water she roared past the Three and pushed into the lead. A minute later she was in the air, and the low hills embracing the bay fell away. Read let his plane soar.

Then on the intercom he called, "Breese, can you see the others?"

A pause, then: "They're still down there."

Stone broke in. "I don't think they can get off, Putty."

"Damn," Read muttered. Then: "Commander to pilots: make a wide port turn. Let's see what's going on."

The Four responded neatly as she took her broad, lazy bank. Read leaned over the side and looked down. The Three and One were still taxiing eastward, but they had dropped speed.

On the Three Jack Towers was furious. He made his way into the hull. "Now what's wrong?"

Richardson bent down from his seat in the pilot's cockpit. "We can't get her up. She's too heavy."

Towers turned on Machinist L. R. Moore. "What happened? Did you take on too much fuel again?"

"No, sir," Moore said, wounded by the accusation. "I was specially careful about that."

"Then what's wrong?"

"We're just too heavy, sir."

"Lavender," Towers said to his radioman, "notify the others. We'll have to go back and dump something."

Pat Bellinger, a hundred yards behind Towers, watched the Three slow down and gave his pilots a signal to cut speed. Before sliding down into the hull, he glanced up and saw the Four pass overhead to the west. "Something's wrong," he announced to his crew members in the hull. "Jack is slowing down."

Lieutenant Harry Sadenwater was busy at his radio. He jotted a message and handed it to Bellinger. Bellinger read it. "They're too heavy; they can't get off."

Bob Christensen, the One's reserve pilot engineer, said, "We were riding pretty deep ourselves."

Bellinger looked at him quickly. "Trouble?"

"I'm not sure. We'll see when we really try to lift."

Bellinger went to his pilots and tugged at Mitscher's leg. "Follow Jack back, Marc."

"Is the trip off?" Mitscher asked.

"I don't know yet." Bellinger lighted a cigarette and returned to his forward cockpit.

Aloft, Read took Towers's message from Radioman Rodd. Glancing at it, he nodded understandingly. "Tell the pilots to keep circling for a while. It'll give us a chance to tune up the engines."

"Still think we're going?" Rodd asked.

Read indicated the radio message. "This doesn't say no."

Reaching its mooring, the Three's engines sighed discouragingly and stopped. Towers had remained in the hull during the taxi back to the *Aroostock*. In his mind, he visualized the puzzled disappointment that must this minute be on the face of every man aboard her, the deflated spirits of the crowds on the shore, the smug triumph of the English fliers; he knew he could not face any of them.

His familiar frown heavy on his brow, he let his eyes dart appraisingly about the hull. They paused on the radio equipment. He said, "Lavender, what does that long-range set weigh?"

Lavender looked at Towers with dismay. "Why?"

"Something's got to go. What does that thing weigh?"

"We can't do without this, Jack." Lavender touched the set protectively. "How are we going to contact people if we get lost?"

"It's my job to see that we don't," Towers said. "Now, come on!"

"About seventy pounds," Lavender estimated sullenly.

"Rip her out."

"It'll be like ripping off my right arm."

"That may have to go, too." Towers resumed his study of the hull. The planes had been designed with such thrift that little could be termed superfluous; every ounce had its job, its duty. Pushed in a corner was a sack of mail philatelist clubs had collected for souvenirs, one bag for each plane. Towers spied it and picked it up; he figured it weighed thirty pounds. "Get rid of this," he said.

Now. What else? Towers examined the hull again, already knowing that what he must do would surely break somebody's heart. But it couldn't be helped. He looked from man to man. The pilots were essential, of course. So was Lavender, even minus one radio. There were two engineers —Machinist Lloyd Moore and Lieutenant Braxton Rhodes.

He would have to do with one. Moore was the smaller man. Towers thought: Why can't everybody be built like Putty Read?

He said: "What do you weigh, Rhodes?"

"No, Commander, no!" Rhodes cried unbelieving.

"I'm sorry. You know the problem."

"This thing weighs over twenty thousand pounds," Rhodes argued. "My hundred and sixty can't make any difference."

"One pound can make a difference," Towers said, trying to be patient.

Rhodes insisted, "But we flew all the way up the coast with me on board—and the radio and Richard Byrd besides."

Towers's patience died. "All right, if you can figure out then why we can't get this tub out of the drink today you can take over command and I'll get off."

The two men glared at each other. Rhodes knew he had no argument; he would have to go. He let the anger seep out of him. "Aye, aye, sir," he said quietly. He moved past Towers in order to climb out through the pilots' cockpit.

Towers stepped aside. He reached out quickly and gave Rhodes a pat on the behind. "I'm sorry, boy."

Rhodes was gone.

Putty Read glanced at his watch. He had been circling the bay for eighteen minutes. On one round he saw equipment being removed from the Three—apparently to diminish weight, he presumed. On another round he saw a crew member crawl out of the Three and slide into a waiting motorboat. Had Towers found it necessary to dump a man? Tough luck. No further messages had come from Towers. Lacking instructions, it was up to Read to make his own decisions. On his intercom he called: "Pilots, take her down. We might as well try to find out what's going on."

The Four landed and taxied close to her sister ships.

Towers heard her and looked at his watch. A message came in on Lavender's short-range radio; he transcribed it and handed it to Towers. It was from Read: "Are we going anywhere today?"

Towers said, "Tell him yes. Tell him we're going to the Azores even if we have to row all the way."

The work was done. Towers looked around the hull once more. There was nothing else he could see that could be dumped. All he could try was to take off again. "All right," he said. "Tell Pat and Putty to follow me out to the stream."

Once again the three planes revved up their engines. Once again they taxied heavily into take-off position. Once again the order came from Towers: "Take-off in one minute." Once again the men exchanged attentive glances. Once again they started their rush down the bay.

Read was the first to leave the water; he held up his hands to signal his pilots to rein in so that he could hold the formation. Then Towers lifted, slowly, slowly. Finally Bellinger got up out of the water—just inches at first, then a few feet. It began to look as though he could go no higher.

VII

THEY FLEW INTO THE GROWING NIGHT.

By the time they reached the sea, Read had climbed to six hundred feet, Towers had an altitude of seventy-five feet, and Bellinger, at ten feet, was so low that he had to leave the bay by the regular ship's channel to avoid the cliffs.

The Navy had requested departure statements from the three commanders and now they were radioed to the world. Towers said: "If hard work on the part of everybody counts for anything, we ought to make a go of it. The machines are in excellent shape and the crews are fine, capable fellows."

108

Read said: "Nothing that we could think of in the way of tests or of precautions has been overlooked and I think we'll turn the trick."

And Bellinger said: "With the help of God and in spite of the devil, we're going to do this little thing."

Now in the air and on the way they all put public relations out of their minds and settled down to business.

It was, by New York time, approximately six o'clock in the evening; Greenwich Mean Time, by which they would keep their logs, put the hour at ten. Stretched out before them on a line to the Azores were twenty-five destroyers. The plan was that ships they passed in daylight would send up smoke both for identification and as a means for the planes to set their course. During the night, the ships, on hearing them, would fire rockets in a shower of recognition, then turn on huge spotlights.

The night was cold, but the men were warmly dressed in their flight suits. Those who worked in the cockpits—the navigators, the pilots and sometimes the engineers—wore goggles to protect their faces against the wind, and they were uncomfortable only when they took off their heavy gloves to make notes. But inside the hulls it was warm, at least relatively so. It was also noisy: the men had to stand close when they spoke and even then they had to shout to be heard; at times they scribbled messages to save their throats.

Read was high and alone. Ahead and far below was Towers. The Four behaved with such smooth perfection that Read had to hold her back in order to let Towers remain in the lead and set the course. Read looked around for Bellinger in the One but could not see him. He wondered if something had gone wrong and Pat had turned back.

They passed over the first destroyer and the second. Up

went the smoke, and the fliers waved at it as if it were a new friend. Up, too, went radio messages of good luck and good flight.

Jim Breese was with Radio Operator Herbert Rodd in the Four, jotting down messages as they arrived. "They keep asking for souvenirs," Rodd said.

"We got no souvenirs," Breese said.

"That's what I keep telling them."

Breese thought about it. "Wait a minute." He scurried aft to the shelf where he kept his own engineer equipment and dug out one of the weather balloons he had taken aboard at Far Rockaway to use as a toilet. "I got a souvenir," he said to Rodd. He relieved himself. "You're next," he said, offering Rodd the balloon.

Rodd laughed. "What a mean trick." He took the balloon.

In the forward cockpit, Read heard the laughter on the intercom as Breese made his way to Smokey Rhoads, to Pilots Stone and Hinton, then to Read himself.

"What's this?" Read asked.

"We're preparing a little souvenir for the boys on the ships," Breese explained. "They all keep asking for one."

"In that?" Read pointed to the swollen balloon.

Breese nodded. "Care to join us?"

"What's in it?"

Breese grinned sheepishly. "Well, you remember why I took these aboard?"

Read laughed first, then he shook his head, then he complied.

Breese returned to Rodd. "Any more requests?"

"We should be on target in five minutes."

"Well," said Breese, "these planes were originally built to be bombers." He laughed and went to the rear cockpit and slid into his seat, next to Rhoads. "Help me tie a knot," he said, and Rhoads did. The bomb was ready. On the intercom, Breese told the pilots, "Give me a count."

Stone and Hinton brought the Four directly in line with the waiting destroyer, then dropped altitude to three hundred feet. "Five," Hinton said, "four, three, two—"

Breese saw the destroyer's tail below him, then midships. A cluster of sailors stood on the forward deck, their eyes on the Four, their arms upstretched. Breese released the souvenir. The wind caught it, held it for a moment, then let it fall in a long, slow arc. The sailors scrambled for the heavy object they saw dropping toward them.

Breese watched his bomb hit directly on target amid the souvenir hunters. He sank back in his seat, clicked on his intercom and announced philosophically: "As long as I live I'll always wonder what those guys called us."

2

Pat Bellinger had no time for games. The One's long drag in Trepassey Bay unnerved him; he was just about to instruct his pilots to cut engines when he became aware of the plane's slight lift. Hopefully he waited for a continued rise, but it did not come. When he saw he was unable to send his plane over the low hills and out to sea with the others, he left the bay via the shipping channel like, he felt, a tugboat.

He could not get speed or altitude. Distressed, he went back to talk to his pilots.

"We've got a bad torque," Marc Mitscher said. "It's the new wing."

Bellinger realized what had happened. The fire at Rockaway had damaged the One's structure so badly that one wing had to be replaced. To save time, a wing was removed from the NC-2, that winds had battered against a pier and knocked out of service. The new wing had one square foot more surface. Now when the wind hit the wing it created a pull to starboard that threatened to send the One into a spin.

"Hard to hold her steady," Barin said.

"How's your wrist?" Bellinger asked. He looked at Barin's bandage.

"I know it's there," Barin said, wincing with pain.

"Do you think you can manage?"

Mitscher left the answer to Barin. "Sure."

"As long as we have this torque it's going to take two men to fly this plane," Bellinger pointed out. "That means very little rest for either of you. So don't be a hero, Lou. If your wrist is bad we'll have to go back."

"We'll keep going," Barin said, warmed by Bellinger's concern.

"Okay."

They kept going. As the One burned fuel she slowly gained altitude—rising in an hour to fifty feet, a hundred feet, two hundred feet. Bellinger still felt uneasy. The northern sea was littered with towering icebergs; he could see them all around, dangerously close. He knew that soon it would be night, and if he could not gain a safer altitude and hold it there was the risk of crashing into one of the menacing ice mountains in the dark. What a disgusting moment in Navy aviation that would be!

In the forward cockpit, Bellinger gave his attention to Byrd's navigation instruments and found he was slightly off course to starboard. In view of the torque, this was to be expected. On the intercom he gave his pilots instructions to correct the drift. Ahead and to port he saw the first destroyer, the smoke pouring from her. As Mitscher and Barin corrected the drift, the One drew in line with the ship and passed her port to port. Bellinger trained his binoculars on the ship. His low altitude made him feel the plane and ship were at the same level.

He commented on the intercom: "That j.g. on the bridge has blue eyes. Now there's a bit of information I wish I weren't in a position to discover."

They kept going.

They rose a little more, to three hundred feet.

Bellinger aimed his binoculars ahead in hopes of sighting the Three and Four. Coming night was turning the sky purple. He could see nothing. Then just as he was about to put aside the glasses he spotted the Four, far ahead, high and to port. He could barely discern the Number 4 on her hull. But he took comfort from it. Bringing up the rear though he was, he was still in the air and in sight of a sister ship. He set the binoculars at his feet, then looked west. The sun was sinking fast into the sea. Somewhere out there was the coast of North America. Somewhere in the thickening purple ahead were the Azores. Somewhere in the blackness to the east was Europe. Somewhere in the gray below were icebergs and the cold sea. Well, at least it was good to have some idea where he was.

He slid down into the hull, crawled past the rows of gas tanks and went to Harry Sadenwater. "Any news from the flag?"

3

Jack Towers was having trouble maintaining radio contact with his co-commanders. Bob Lavender knew why: the short-range radio was proving unreliable and the Three's long-range radio was in a stockroom aboard the *Aroostock*, back at Trepassey. To point out that the plight had resulted from Towers's own decision to dump equipment in order to lose weight struck Lavender as both unnecessary and unwise. He would have to do the best he could.

There were enough other problems. When the sun sank and night came, the Three's pilots discovered they could not read their instrument panel. The special paint that was supposed to absorb light by day in order to glow in the dark of night did not work. Dick Richardson repeatedly shone his flashlight on the dials, but within two or three minutes the illuminated effect faded out. Furthermore, the compass was broken, spinning like a top. Altitude, speed, even direction, were matters of guesswork for precious minutes at a time.

"We should have made some night tests," Richardson said to Dave McCulloch. "We would have found out about all this."

"Too late for regrets," McCulloch said. "Thank God we've got the destroyers below to keep us headed in the right direction, at least."

"As long as we've got the visibility to see them," Richardson observed sadly. "Look."

They were approaching a broad field of clouds.

On the intercom, Towers asked, "What's our altitude?"

"Seven hundred feet," Richardson replied.

"It's getting lumpy," Towers said. "Ascend above those clouds."

Richardson pulled back on his stick and increased speed. He could feel the plane breathe deep and start to climb. In a few minutes he informed Towers, "Twelve hundred feet, Commander."

"Steady," said Towers. Then: "Captain to radio. Request reports from the One and Four."

"I'll try," Lavender muttered. He tapped out his questions.

114

Read reported that he was at two thousand feet, estimated five miles behind the Three. Bellinger put himself at eight hundred feet, some ten miles behind Read.

Towers instructed, "All planes turn on running lights."

Read and Bellinger passed the instructions on to their engineers. On went the lights: a white light at the leading edge of the upper wing on the center line; green and red lights on the starboard and port outboard struts.

Bellinger radioed: "I can see one of you, up high."

Read queried: "NC-4 to NC-3. Are your lights on? I don't see you."

There was a quiet moment, then the Three replied, "Apparently our lights are not functioning. Keep your distance."

Lavender received Read's acknowledgment, but he did not hear from Bellinger. When Lavender repeatedly failed to reach Sadenwater, he asked Rodd on the Four to relay the message about the broken running lights on the Three. Now Sadenwater did not respond. But Lavender picked up:

"NC-4, if that's you on top, blink your eyes."

"NC-1, we are flickering our running lights, as requested."

"We see you. Thanks."

"Welcome. The flag says her lights are busted. Watch it."

"Will do."

Well, at least they both knew.

A few minutes after midnight, Greenwich time, the moon came up, amazingly big and bright. It rose quickly and showed that the cloud formation was actually in three layers. Depending on its altitude, each crew saw a different slice of the moon. Admiring the moonlight, Dick Richardson saw its rays reflect off the Three's wings and send a rainbow against the clouds.

He brought it to McCulloch's attention, and said, "I didn't know there were rainbows at night."

Dave McCulloch glanced at it evenly. "You learn something new every day."

There were few stars. Read noticed that when he went up to four thousand feet in search of smoother air; he had expected to see many of them. The smoother air he had also expected failed to materialize and after a few minutes he decided to go down again. His major concern was accurate navigation; for that he would have to rely greatly on the patrol ships, and he was afraid that, so high above the clouds, he would not see their burst of shells, nor would they be able to catch him in their spotlights. Since the ride was apparently going to be a bumpy one at any level, he preferred to take his bumps at a safer altitude.

Pat Bellinger had discovered his own kind of comfort. Hours in the air had diminished the One's fuel supply enough to provide a quick response to controls. Bellinger felt better knowing he could rise or drop, according to his judgments. Also, despite the pulling torque, Mitscher and Barin were managing to keep the plane steady. Pat was aware of the agony they were going through, especially Barin with his bad wrist, but they were both content with their progress and neither man took time away from the controls to rest. And they were making good speed, holding easily at seventy and seventy-five miles an hour, occasionally spurting to as fast as ninety. At times the strong, variable wind swung around and shoved them over a hundred miles an hour. Dazzled by these gusts of record speed, Mitscher and Barin would grin at each other proudly.

Richardson was not so pleased with the sudden bursts. His panel darkened, he was often unsure of what was happening to the Three, and he did not like that. He kept in constant intercom contact with Towers in the bow and Lavender at the radio in order to be always informed. Anxiously, he counted off the destroyers as they passed below, knowing that each one meant he was closer to the Azores. The thick clouds made him uneasy. They had not been forecast; the weather was supposed to be clear all the way.

Towers was equally uneasy. The clouds interfered with his use of Byrd's drift indicator. A major factor of the equipment was the torch that was dropped to the water; by day it gave off smoke and by night it gave off a bright glow, and by either the navigator could compute the drift of his plane from its course. Now the heavy clouds and patches of fog required the navigator-commanders to drop low, often less than fifty feet, in order to keep the torches in sight. Flying without running lights and with poor visibility, he recognized the danger in the vertical movements the three planes had to make at a time when he had trouble seeing the Four and One and he knew they could not see him at all.

His fears were justified around three in the morning. The clouds had unexpectedly parted and the moon sent a shaft of light down to the sea. McCulloch came on the intercom. "Commander, I see somebody below us. I think it's the Four."

Towers reached for his binoculars and leaned out of his cockpit. "It's the Four, all right." She was less than five hundred feet below, maybe a hundred feet ahead, and holding steady.

"Should we warn her?" McCulloch suggested.

Towers had lost trust in his radio. "No. Let's go up a thousand feet and two points to port."

The Three began to take its new position.

Suddenly from Machinist Rasmus Christensen in the rear cockpit came the cry, "Good God!"

Towers looked up. Out of the thick clouds came the One, aimed directly at the Three, but just fifty feet above her.

There was no time to do anything. The One skimmed the structure of the Three for the instant they were at passing altitude and then was gone into the darkness.

Jack Towers let himself drop back into the hull, then he stood for a moment at his work table, gripping it tensely. He waited until composure returned, then made his way to Lavender. "Try to reach them, and if you can't, instruct the destroyers to relay the message. Tell them to stop making any effort to stay in sight of each other. From now on, each man is on his own. But I want a report on their locations every five minutes; if we can't acknowledge, they can check with the destroyers. And tell Pat the last time I saw him—and it was close—he was on too southerly a course. Got that?"

"Yes, sir," Lavender said.

It had indeed been close. With all that room up there, with only three planes in the air over the Atlantic, two of them had almost collided. The thought made Towers shudder. He sighed heavily. "I don't want anything like that to happen again."

It didn't. It couldn't. In a very short time the air over the Atlantic was tragically cleared of the planes that were trying to conquer it.

VIII

ABRUPTLY AT five-forty-five in the morning, Greenwich time, dawn came full. The discomfort of night flying faded with it. Read had not slept all night, but he was not tired. He remembered, however, that he hadn't eaten since noon of the day before. In the hull he found the thermos of coffee and took a cup. He also ate a ham sandwich and a candy bar. He noticed that the food, for the most part, had been untouched, but he could understand this. In his years of flying he had observed that there was always a certain tension while in the air that dimmed appetites; usually it was only after a landing that crews realized how hungry they were. On this flight it had been the same with sleep. By plan, each man was to have a few minutes every hour for a nap but none of them took full advantage of it. If a man stretched out at all, even shut his eyes, he remained alert for the slightest sound or movement that might indicate trouble. Well, it was morning now. The first experience of night flying was over. They could all relax.

Dick Richardson felt the same relief. By plan, the pilots were to spell each other every half-hour, but it didn't work out that way. The Three kept running into turbulence that required both pilots at the controls. Richardson would handle the ailerons and watch the wing tips in order to keep the plane level; McCulloch handled the rudder and the elevator and tried to keep the plane on course. Even in calm moments neither pilot left his seat for more than a few seconds—both men quietly anxious to know what was happening at all times.

With dawn, Richardson relaxed. After an hour of it, he felt the need to stretch. He went into the hull for the exercise of letting his arms and legs reach out full length and he felt better. Back in his seat, the cold air and the steady hum of the engines began to lull him to sleep. He remembered the medical kit the Navy doctors had prepared; in it were capsules of strychnine and caffein to be taken as stimulants to throw off just such sudden sieges of fatigue. He returned to the hull and took a dose. It didn't work. At the controls he started to react more slowly and less accurately.

Dave McCulloch watched him, worried. At last he called Towers on the intercom. "Something's wrong with Dick. He can't stay awake. Maybe he needs some of the strychnine."

"I just saw him take a dose," Towers said.

"Well, he's practically asleep up here."

"Send him down," Towers said.

Richardson obeyed McCulloch's nudge like a sleepy child.

He slid back into the hull, losing his balance and almost falling. He tried to smile, but his muscles would not respond. He gave Towers a dazed, silly look.

Towers fixed a double dose of the stimulant. "I want you to take this, Dick," he said. "We'll be in shortly and we'll need every man wide-awake."

Richardson took the dose numbly. Towers stood near, watching. Richardson could not keep his eyes open. Then, slowly, his blood carried the jolt through his system; he felt the tingling in his toes and finger tips and the back of his neck. His knees and elbows itched.

"Is it working?" Towers asked.

"I think so. Is there any coffee?"

"You couldn't get any more caffein into you if you had five pounds of coffee."

The heaviness drained out of him. A big yawn cleared his head. "I'm all right now. That must be powerful stuff."

"You won't need any sleep for three days."

This was good, because he wasn't going to get any.

2

Around ten o'clock in the morning—it was near six in New York—the fog and rain began. This was entirely unexpected. The forecast of clear weather for at least thirty-six hours was apparently wrong. By now, the three planes were more than two-thirds of their way to the Azores. They were all off course, though not seriously. To escape the bad weather, they had all gone aloft, as high as four thousand feet, but in doing so they lost visual contact with the destroyers that marked the route for them. They also were unable to use Byrd's navigation instruments from that altitude. Since daylight, the bursting shells and spotlights on the destroyers were not effective. It became increasingly vital for each navigator to know his specific location. The Azores were small and could easily be missed. Furthermore, the islands had dangerous high mountains—which might not be missed.

Bellinger went down for a look. At six hundred feet, he saw Destroyer Number 17, the *Stockton*, twelve miles off on the port band. He gave instructions to Barin and Mitscher to correct the error in their course. In the process of doing so, they ran into fog so thick that it clogged their goggles and blacked out their panel board.

"Let's get out of this!" Mitscher called on the intercom. "Take her up!"

They rose quickly to three thousand feet, again losing contact with the surface but at least able to see ahead.

Near seven in the morning, Read spotted a freighter below him, a comforting sight. Running ahead of the others, Read sensed the turn in the weather earlier, around eight. Anxious to stay on course, he was reluctant to ascend to a smoother altitude at the risk of losing visual contact with the important destroyers. He therefore continued at a steady level. He ran into rain and patches of thick fog, but as each passed quickly he held to his decision to maintain his altitude.

An hour later he was not so confident. Now the fog was very thick. He passed over Destroyer 16, the *Hopewell*, and was astonished by how close he had come to not seeing her. He radioed ahead to the *Stockton* for a visibility report and was told there was no visibility at all at sea level.

According to his speed, he could reach the *Stockton's* position in approximately fifty minutes. "I'm going up," he informed the ship by radio, "and will look for you later."

He plugged in his headphone at Rodd's radio table and said, "Navigator to pilots." He got no answer. He tried again.

Still no answer. He said to Rodd, "Is this thing working?" Rodd gave no indication that he heard Read. Read tapped his shoulder. "Is the intercom working?"

Rodd looked at him, frowned, then said, "I can't hear you." He lifted the earflap of his helmet.

Read leaned over and shouted, "See if you can contact the pilots." Rodd tried, but without luck. He tried reaching Breese and Rhoads in the aft cockpit, but again without luck. The intercom was broken.

Read went to the pilots' cockpit and tugged at Stone's leg and indicated with gestures that he wanted to see his log. In a margin, Read wrote: "The intercom is out. Get up above this fog."

Stone read the note, nodded and gave Hinton a thumbs-up. The Four climbed to 3,200 feet, into the clear.

Read took the log again and wrote: "Watch me for signals. In approx. 45 min. drop for course check on 17."

He went forward to his work table. The intercom was broken again; it meant the inconvenience of running back and forth in the hull and writing notes to make his decisions known. As long as there were no emergencies, the inconvenience would be a bore, but it would be critical if he had to write a note in circumstances where there wouldn't be time to finish it.

He climbed into his cockpit and looked at his compass. At least they were headed in the right direction, if possibly not on the right course.

Meanwhile, Towers knew he was off course. Just before entering the storm area, he made a fix on Destroyer 13, the *Bush*. Two hours later his calculations put him between Numbers 17 and 18, the *Stockton* and the *Craven*, but he could not be sure. Around noon, the Three rose above the clouds long enough for Towers to get a look at the sun. New calculations indicated that he was well off course, to the south.

He instructed Lavender, "Contact some of the ships and see if you can work out a radio fix on our position." Then he sent for Machinist Lloyd Moore. "How much fuel do we have left?"

"About two hours," Moore said.

Too little. "We can't fool around," Towers observed. He called Richardson on the intercom. "Change course to ninety degrees magnetic."

"Aye, aye, sir," Richardson said easily. He thought he sensed uncertainty in Towers's voice. He waited.

Then: "Dick, I can't figure it. We should be there by now."

"Yes, sir?"

"We're off course, south, but even so . . ."

Richardson waited.

Towers said, "I've asked Lavender to get a radio compass bearing. That won't be easy as long as we keep moving."

"Do you want to sit down?"

"Do you think we can?"

"Dave and I parked this plane once before, off Delaware."

"In a soup like this?"

"No, but . . ." He wanted the decision to be Towers's.

"Let's go down and take a look."

At the same time, Bellinger was considering the same action. At three thousand feet, the One was side-slipping badly. Strong winds that shifted vigorously spun the plane around helplessly. After two hours of this, Bellinger realized he was completely lost. Like Towers, he gave up with his own navigation instruments and told his radioman to try

124

to get a bearing from the ships below. When this failed, he instructed his pilots to drop as low as they could to see if there was enough visibility at the surface to use Byrd's instruments to establish their drift. The One descended to seventy-five feet. In clear patches, visibility was less than a half-mile, scarcely enough room to use the drift indicator.

Read, too, was ready to descend. By his watch, the Four had covered enough distance to go down and look for the *Stockton*. Read raised his arm to catch Stone's attention; getting it, Read motioned downward. The Four began to glide.

He glanced at his compass and gasped: it was spinning crazily. In an instant, he had lost all sense of direction. He felt a strong wind against his face and looked at his speedometer: the Four was traveling twenty miles an hour faster than it should be. A look at his altimeter showed, oddly, that the plane was not losing height. But what was wrong?

Clouds cleared for a moment and Read saw the sun. He also saw that the port wing had dipped and the plane was whirling in a tight circle like a top. Unless the plane leveled soon it could plunge into a nose dive.

What was the matter with Stone? Couldn't he see what was happening? Was he so preoccupied with his instruments that he hadn't noticed he had let the port wing drop?

The speed and wind and spinning trapped Read in his cockpit. He struggled to get out so that he could rush through the hull to Stone. Helplessly he waved his arms, but Stone was not looking at him. Where was Hinton? Read could not see him; he must be in the hull, unaware, by the phenomenon of flight, of what was going on.

The clouds cleared again. Puzzled to feel the sun upon him when, by now, he should be deep in the storm, Stone looked around. He saw the dipped wing. He grabbed at the controls and leveled the plane. The Four shot above the clouds into the clear.

Read sank back, panting. His impulse was to rush to Stone in fury, but he knew this would do no good. And there was no time for it. According to the compass, they were now headed for Pittsburgh. Read made speedy calculations and tumbled through the hull to shove new orders into Stone's hand. He stood still as he felt the plane bank to the new course. He sighed heavily a few times, letting his anger seep out of him and his shock calm. If the intercom had been working he might have ripped into Stone for his carelessness, but to do so in the circumstances meant he would either have to shout his head off or write a fast book.

He stopped at Rodd's side and scribbled: "Notify No. 17 we won't descend for check. Ask ahead for visibility."

He waited for the answers. Destroyer 19, the *Dent,* reported a thick fog; Number 20, the *Philip,* said it was in a heavy mist; Number 21, the *Waters,* the last ship before the Azores, announced, "Visibility ten miles."

It was over two hundred miles to the *Waters.* Read jotted: "Tell them we'll keep at present altitude."

Miles apart and completely unaware of what was happening to each other, Jack Towers and Pat Bellinger made fateful and similar decisions.

Bellinger was at seventy-five feet and in dense fog. He said to his pilots, "If this doesn't clear in a few minutes, let's land." The fog did not clear.

Towers was at five hundred feet. He called to Richardson: "How does it look to you?"

Richardson leaned over his cockpit and examined the sea. "Not bad, Commander."

But it was not the sea he was looking at. The fog, so

thick that it seemed solid, had settled upon the surface and hid waves that soared to sixty feet.

"All right," Towers said. "You're driving. Park whenever you're ready."

And Bellinger said, "We're lost, Marc. Take her down and let's see if we can pick up a radio bearing."

It was shortly after one o'clock in the afternoon, fifteen hours by Greenwich time from the departure from Trepassey.

The One landed first; the Three a few minutes after her. The One crashed into a rising wave; a solid roof of raging sea crushed down on her and buried her in a deep trough. Up she went again on the crest of a new wave, her tail caught in the wash. The Three hit the crest of a wave, shuddered savagely, then skimmed across to another crest. The second wave spun her around, then dropped her, dead weight, into a fifty-foot trough.

The men aboard both planes heard the crunch of struts, the snap of wires, the bark of snapping wood.

They all knew they would never be able to take off again. They wondered how long it would be before the hulls began to break up.

IX

THE ONE'S engines were still running as she settled. They forced the plane to fight back at the sea, battering futilely at the waves. Bellinger, crouched in his cockpit, gave himself an instant for pains and aches to start, but none came. He ducked in the hull and went to the pilots. "Keep the forward engine running but cut the others," he hollered above the wind. Then he realized that he was drenched and that he was standing in two feet of water.

"Where's Christy?" he shouted aft.

Christensen came toward him.

"Start the pumps, Christy, and get this stuff out of here."

Mitscher came down from his cockpit. "Is everybody all right?"

"I guess so," Bellinger said. "You?"

"We're okay. We're stuck here, Pat. We'll never get up."

"I know." Bellinger turned to Sadenwater. "How's your set?"

"It seems to be working."

"Keep sending an SOS."

Sadenwater bent over his key.

Bellinger said, "Let's look at the damage." They went aft, passing Christensen and Kesler at work on the bilge pumps, and crawled up into the rear cockpit. Topside, they saw that several wing struts were broken, letting the wings sink low; waves swept across the wings, pulling the whole plane deep into the water. The tail beams were snapped and the loose tail swung in the wind.

They went below. Bellinger said, "Kesler, take a knife and go up and slash the wing fabric so the water can get through." Kesler nodded and put on the work belt by which he could hook himself to the superstructure for safety. Bellinger asked Sadenwater, "Any luck?"

"I can hear them but apparently they can't hear me," Sadenwater said.

"What are they saying?"

"They're pretty sure we're down."

"We sure are."

"They think that Towers is down, too."

"And Putty?"

"Nobody knows."

"Keep trying." Bellinger turned to Mitscher again. "Can Lou handle the controls by himself?"

"There's not much to handle."

"Then give me a hand. Let's put out some sea anchors so the wind stops knocking us around. Christy, are the pumps working all right?"

"Just starting to catch," Christensen replied.

"Help us here, then."

The bulky bundles of canvas, once secured to the hull by ropes and then thrown overboard, were intended to fill with water and serve as anchors. The three men tossed one anchor from the bow and two from stern. For a moment the plane stopped twisting in the wind, but then the strong sea grabbed at the anchors and snapped their ropes like thread. The anchors sank.

Bellinger cursed, then asked quietly, "Who the devil designed those things?"

2

Towers was wondering the same thing. The ropes on his anchors broke even before the canvas bags were full. He was in more serious trouble than Bellinger. On landing, his forward engine struts buckled and the engine sank a foot out of position. The flying wires went slack, and so did the aileron wires. The hull was leaking; several longitudinals and frames had cracked. A hull truss wire had been swept away and the tubular struts that connected the wing engines to the hull were badly bent.

After learning that everyone had taken the landing without injury, Towers's next concern was radio contact. The power for the short range radio—all he had—was derived from the propeller action of the forward engine, now beyond use.

"Can we relocate the generator to another engine, Dinty?" Towers asked Machinist Lloyd Moore.

130

"I think so," Moore said.

"It won't be any fun out there," Towers warned.

Moore shrugged. "It has to be done." He put on his work belt, heavy with tools, and prepared to go topside. He paused and looked soberly at Towers. "Sir, if anything happens to me out there—I mean, if I go overboard, just forget it. You won't be able to pick me up in this storm, so don't even try."

"Be careful," Towers said.

Moore went on deck through the rear cockpit and crawled quickly to the superstructure. Richardson and McCulloch had turned the plane into the northwest wind in order to control her better. They heard Moore behind them and looked to see what he was doing. With gestures, Moore indicated his job. The pilots nodded, understanding. They worked harder to hold the plane steady.

Latching his belt to the struts, Moore knelt and began to unscrew the generator from the wing. The wind was strong and cold. Rain and waves drenched him. His fingers went numb and he had to work slowly. It took him almost forty-five minutes to free the generator. He decided to use the port engine and cautiously made his way to it, wrapping his legs around one strut for support as, with his free hand, he reached out for the next. In a half-hour the generator was attached, then Moore spent another fifteen minutes assuring that the connections were proper. He returned to the hull.

"Okay. Try it."

Towers gave Richardson orders to start the engine. "Easy. The foundation is damaged."

Richardson turned on the engine, keeping it low. He noticed that even at a thousand revolutions it drove the plane diagonally across the sea, decreasing his control. "I don't want to do more than this," he called down to Towers.

Towers asked Lavender, "Getting any power?"

Lavender checked his gauges. "Two amps. About two and a half."

"That gives you a good radius. See what you can pick up."

Lavender began his SOS, pausing intermittently to listen. "They're not getting me," he said.

"Who've you got?" Towers asked.

"The *Columbia*."

According to plan, the destroyer was in the channel between Fayal and Pico, inner islands of the Azores.

Towers said, "Hold on to her and see if you can get a fix."

Lavender twisted dials with his left hand while making notations with his right. In a minute he handed Towers his reading. Towers went forward to his charts and worked for several moments. He came back. "I figure we're forty-five miles southwest of Corvo."

Corvo, westernmost of the principal Azores, was to be the first landmark on the flight's true course. If Towers was right, the Three was also south of Flores, the major island east of Corvo, but almost at the same longitude with Fayal. The wind was pushing the plane toward the islands. Ahead were fierce currents, reefs, rocky shores.

Towers asked: "You still hear the *Columbia?*"

"Spotty," Lavender said.

"What's she say?"

"I don't think she knows we're down. They're trying to pick up our radio from the *Dent* or the *Philip*."

That was miles north. "Damn."

"I think the One is down."

"Are you sure?"

"She reported that she was going to land for a compass check. They haven't heard from her since."

"What about Putty?"

"They haven't mentioned the Four. But they keep talking about a search for two planes. And they don't know we're down."

3

Putty Read looked at his watch, unaware that at this very moment the One and Three were down, their crews struggling for survival. Three hours had passed since he had sighted one of the destroyers, three hours since he had been able to fix his location in the storm-racked sky. He was at 3,400 feet, between two banks of clouds. The wind had shifted again, but he could only guess what it was doing to his plane. He sensed he was being blown off course, to the southeast, but he was not sure. His one certainty was that he was getting low on gas and that he would have to land soon, somewhere.

He watched the clouds carefully. Those above were a thick blanket. Those below churned like the sea itself. He had been informed that the visibility ahead was good. His eyes restlessly upon the clouds below him, he searched for hints of it.

Then it happened. The clouds below parted and, leaning over the port side, Read saw beneath him a sudden darkness of the water: a tide rip. He knew that this agitation of cross currents seldom occurred far from land. They must be near.

He turned around and waved his arms at his pilots, then gestured for them to descend. The Four entered the lower clouds and took a severe buffeting as it lost altitude. Through rifts in the fog, Read was able to keep his eye on the tide rip. Suddenly he glimpsed the outline of a huge rock.

He said aloud, "That's no tide rip—it's a surf line."

Afraid that he might be so close to one of the islands that the plane could strike a mountain, he signaled the pilots to make a complete turn and continue their descent to seaward. At two hundred feet they escaped the clouds.

There it was: an island, a big one.

Read studied it quickly, closely, then ducked down to his charts to check for landmarks. It was Flores, the south coast of it. They were coming into it from the west, which meant they were almost fifty miles off course. But they were over the Azores, and that was all that mattered.

They rounded a point and saw a peaceful farmhouse, set in the midst of cultivated fields. It was like a glance at Heaven. Read was very happy. Even if something went wrong now and they were forced down, they were surrounded by islands and could make it to shore somehow.

According to plan, their destination was Ponta Delgada, the capital of the Azores, on São Miguel Island, 250 miles away. At their present altitude, visibility was good; Read estimated he could see ten or twelve miles.

He went aft and found Jim Breese perched in the engineers' cockpit, enjoying the view. He nudged Breese and motioned for him to come into the hull.

Backing him against the hull, Read shouted into Breese's ear, "How's the fuel?"

Breese made an O with his fingers. "Plenty."

"Can we make about three hundred miles?"

"Easy."

"We're doing about eighty miles. We should make it in about four hours."

Breese grinned and made the O again.

Read grinned. He wanted to hug somebody but his New England reticence kept him from it. He went back to his cockpit.

He sighted Destroyer Number 22 and guided his plane directly over it, low. He could see the cheering, jumping sailors on the deck. He set his course for Destroyer 23, halfway to Horta, on the island of Fayal; there would be two more ships in the next expanse of sea to Ponta Delgada.

Part way to Fayal, the wind changed again and the dense fog came back. Read missed the twenty-third patrol ship. The mountains were his major fear. If he got off his course again, there was every possibility of running into one; they were all around him. He wanted desperately to reach Ponta Delgada, but not so much that he was willing to risk his men for it. As the Four groaned eastward, Read considered his situation and made a decision. The *Columbia* was at Horta. His charts put Horta—Fayal Island—to his south. If the fog did not clear in ten minutes, he would turn south and land at Fayal. There was too much danger involved to try anything else.

He divided his attention between his watch and the fog ahead. Ten minutes passed. There was no improvement. He caught Hinton's eye and signaled him to make a ninety-degree right turn. After the turn, he ordered a gradual descent. Soon the north shore of Fayal was briefly visible below them. They crossed the island and went out to sea, then made a wide turn and came back at the southern coast, low and slow.

Read was not acquainted with the island, and since no stop had originally been planned there he had no accurate map of the coastline. Horta, he assumed, would be on a deep bay. Watching the fogbound coastline, he sighted what he took to be the Horta bight. With hand signals, he guided the Four gently down to the water and to a landing. The pilots taxied into the bay. There was no town.

Breese crawled up on the deck. "What are we doing here?" he called to Read.

"Looking for Horta."

Breese stretched and looked around. "I don't see anything but a few farms."

"We're in the wrong bight," Read said, annoyed. "Let's go up again."

The mistake had cost them four minutes. Hinton and Stone turned the Four around and took off toward the sea. Gaining altitude, they banked to the east and crossed a short peninsula. The fog cleared for an instant. There was Horta. There was the *Columbia*.

They landed, fifteen hours and eighteen minutes out of Trepassey. The worst was over for them—for now.

4

For Bellinger and the men on the One, the worst was still ahead. Trapped in the storm that raged northwest of the Azores, he had no control over his plane and no contact with the world. Each wave that swamped the plane sent another foot of water into the hull. The bilge pumps coughed and sputtered, unable to keep up with their job. Bellinger ordered Harry Sadenwater to remain at his radio; the rest of the crew was put to work bailing. Marc Mitscher was violently ill, the smell of his vomit heavy in the dank hull.

"Marc, go topside and get some air," Bellinger said in a voice of pity tinged with impatience. "You can't do much here."

"I can't do much there either," Mitscher said.

"Go ahead."

Mitscher obeyed, understanding.

The bailing went on. After an hour of it, the men had lowered the water level to their knees, and in another hour they had it at their ankles. But they could not get all of it out. For protection, strips of canvas had been fixed to the rear and forward cockpits, but new waves repeatedly ripped them away, flooding the cabin again. The chore was endless but it was vital; with too much water weight inside, the hull would sink.

In the third hour, Kesler found the food supply. The invading sea had chilled the coffee Thermos to bitterness. The ham sandwiches were salt-soaked. The chocolate was mud. Tins of emergency rations had been taken aboard, and the crew resorted to these. They were tasteless, but they eased the hunger pains of men who had not eaten for almost twenty-four hours and who had worked hard for the past three.

The plane rose and sank, rolled, twisted, yawed. Now Christensen got sick. Up came the rations he had eaten. Helpless, he let his weary body sink into the filthy bilge and hung his head between his legs.

Sadenwater remained at his radio, tapping out an endless SOS.

At the controls, Lou Barin scanned the close horizon with aching eyes. Suddenly he let out a yell and stamped his feet on the floorboard. "Ship! Ship! A ship!"

There was panic in the hull. Bellinger rushed forward to his cockpit, ripped away the canvas and lifted himself high—just in time to be beaten back by a brutal wave. He sank to his knees, gulped, spat, tasted vomit in his throat, then forced himself back into the cockpit.

He saw it—a freighter—more than a mile to starboard. He rushed back into the hull for his Very pistol, to shoot off a rocket, but the weapon was wet and would not work. He returned to the cockpit and started to holler. Lou Barin hollered from his position. Christensen and Kesler hollered from the rear cockpit. Sadenwater pressed heavily on his wireless key, as if his own muscles could make the radio louder.

The fog closed in. The freighter disappeared. They were alone again.

It had been a cruel moment, with hope so briefly alive. Gathered again in the hull at the radio, the men could not look at each other, could not speak. It had been cruel.

It was six o'clock. They had been in the water five hours. Soon it would be night, night of a day that had seen little daylight. To sustain them, the crew had only three tins of rations and three of the five gallons of drinking water they had taken on at Trepassey. The men were tired, very tired; cold, painfully cold. Their spirits were completely deflated; two of the men were so sick they did not care what happened to them. And night was coming.

"We'll have to post a watch," Bellinger said wearily. "In case another ship—" he began to explain, then decided it wasn't necessary.

His men looked at him, waiting.

"We'll have to have one pilot at the controls," he went on, "for what little maneuverability we have. Marc, how do you feel?" Mitscher groaned. "Do you think you can take the first watch? Lou's been up there for hours."

"Sure," Mitscher said. "Sure."

"I'll take it with you," Bellinger offered. "Christy, you take the second watch with Lieutenant Barin."

"Yes, sir."

Bellinger looked at Sadenwater, then asked, "Kesler, do you know Morse?"

"A little."

"Do you know the SOS?"

"Yes, sir, I know that."

"Good. Then you spell Lieutenant Sadenwater at the radio for a while. If you get anything, wake him up. But just keep sending the SOS."

"Yes, sir."

Mitscher said, "Pat, it isn't necessary to have two men in the cockpit. There's not that much work to do."

"I don't want anybody falling asleep up there," Bellinger explained. "One good wave, and a man can be in the drink. Besides, there's too much ocean for one man to keep an eye on it all."

That settled it.

"Okay," said Bellinger. "Let's go, Marc. Four hours."

Barin came down from the cockpit and was briefed; he agreed the watch was a good idea. Mitscher and Bellinger climbed into the section and tried to make themselves comfortable. The seat was soaked, but so were they and they did not mind.

Four thousand feet up, the sun still shone, but on the sea it was already night. Unexpectedly the fog would part and a shaft of sunlight would break through, first a mile away, then five miles away, then on the plane itself, briefly, brightly, eerily. The plane bobbed and dipped and slid down the sides of sudden waves. Mitscher sat stiffly in his seat, gray and glum. Bellinger watched the monotonous, restless sea.

The blast from the freighter came across the surface at them like cannon fire. Startled, Bellinger jumped, cracking his knees against the panel board. Mitscher broke into a sweat. Belowdeck there was a sudden scramble. The freighter was behind them, about a half-mile. A lifeboat was being lowered over the side. Struggling to hold her safe distance, the big ship swung around and Bellinger could see her name: the *Ionia,* out of Athens.

In an instant, Christy and Kesler were in the rear cockpit, Barin and Sadenwater up forward, all watching the lifeboat and cheering her in. She was alongside in five minutes, her rope in Kesler's grip.

As commander, Bellinger had two duties: he should be the last to leave his damaged plane, but he should also be the first to greet the captain of the rescue ship.

"I wonder if we can save the plane?" he asked Mitscher.

"How?"

"Maybe the *Ionia* can tow us into port."

"It'll be hard to secure a rope in this sea," Mitscher said.

Bellinger made up his mind. "Let's go aboard and ask the skipper if he's willing to try."

The crew of the NC-1 left their plane and climbed into the lifeboat. Under cautious power, the *Ionia* allowed the sea to draw her nearer. In a few minutes, Bellinger and his men were aboard the freighter, and he was in for a surprise.

He saluted the Greek Captain and shook his hand and said, "Thank you very much, sir. We were afraid nobody was picking up our distress call."

The Greek officer accepted the handshake and returned the triumphant smile and replied with: "No Eenglish." He grinned good-naturedly and held up his hands helplessly.

Bellinger understood. "Radio," he said. He cupped one hand in another and pretended to send code. "Dit-dit-dit-dat-dat-dat—"

Comprehension dawned on the Greek's face. He shook his head again. "No. No." He pointed up at the ship's superstructure. There were no antennas. The ship had no radio.

Bellinger was baffled. "How did you find us?"

The Captain was helpless again and his half-smile showed it.

Bellinger turned to the First Mate. "English? Anybody?"

The Mate took up his captain's embarrassed laughter. "No," he said, and ruled out the rest of the crew with a wide gesture.

Bellinger tried again. He gestured to the Captain, then to himself, then to the sea and his plane, then put a question of puzzlement on his face.

Now the Captain understood and again his laughter was triumphant. He put a finger to his eye. "So. So." He pointed to his watch and held up two fingers.

So he had seen them two hours before, and had been hunting for them ever since. Bellinger found himself grateful for the dignity of the sea that led mariners to make such dangerous sacrifices for the sake of strangers.

"Now," he said, "how do I make him understand that I want him to tow the plane?"

He saw a rope on the deck, picked it up, slung it over his shoulder and went through a pulling motion. Then he indicated the ship, pointed out to his plane, blown by the wind to within three hundred yards, held up the rope and looked at the Captain with a pleading expression.

Again the Captain understood. The lifeboat was just about to be raised. The Captain gave his orders and the boat was untied from its pulleys. Another order from the Captain sent the freighter into slow reverse, maneuvering toward the NC-1. Soon the big freighter towered over the crippled plane. A rope was thrown down to the lifeboat crew and they tied it to the One's bow. Once more the Captain gave an order; the *Ionia* began to glide forward. The rope broke and the One bobbed away. They tried again, this time at-

141

taching the rope to the One's wings. But as the ship moved out the wing snapped and the rope fell into the water.

The Captain touched Bellinger's arm and pointed out to sea. There, more than a mile out, Bellinger recognized the blinking of an Aldis lamp. He called: "Sadenwater, who is that?"

Sadenwater read the message. "It's the *Gridley*. They're asking about us."

The Greek Captain touched Bellinger's arm again, this time pointing up to the *Ionia*'s bridge where another lamp was attached to a railing.

"Come on, Harry," Bellinger said, and he led Sadenwater quickly to the bridge. "Give them the news."

Sadenwater flashed: "NC-1 CREW ABOARD THE IONIA, ALL SAFE AND SOUND."

The *Gridley* replied: "THANK GOD. OUR CONGRATULATIONS AND GRATITUDE TO HER SKIPPER. WHERE'S SHE BOUND?"

Bellinger felt his now familiar helplessness with his rescuer. Impulsively, he led the Captain into the *Ionia*'s pilot room and to the map table. Without having to ask, he saw that the ship was out of Norfolk en route to Portugal. Bellinger pointed to the Azores. "Ponta Delgada?"

The Captain shook his head and pointed to Portugal. "Lisbon."

Bellinger returned to Sadenwater. "Tell them Lisbon."

The *Gridley* replied: "SUGGEST MOVING IN TO TAKE YOU ABOARD. ANY INSTRUCTIONS?"

"Tell them we're trying to tow the plane," said Bellinger.

Sadenwater sent the message. The *Gridley* suggested: "LET US GIVE IT A TRY."

Because of the fog, it took almost an hour for the *Gridley* to approach to a safe distance and send out her own small boats to pick up Bellinger and his crew. Bellinger could think of no way to communicate his gratitude to the *Ionia*'s captain except repeated salutes and handshakes as he left the freighter. Boarding the *Gridley* was like reaching home. The familiar sights and sounds and smells were good enough to be a dream. After the *Ionia* pulled away, the *Gridley* attempted to take the NC-1 in tow, but each effort failed, each time the plane broke up more.

At last the Captain of the *Gridley* said, "We can't do it, and we can't stay out here much longer trying."

"That's a shame," Bellinger said.

"But we can't just leave her there either," the Captain said. "She's a menace to shipping. We'll have to sink her."

Bellinger pursed his lips in regret. Yet he knew there was nothing he could do. The *Gridley* turned and went full steam at the NC-1, hitting her square and sending her to the bottom.

It had been Marc Mitscher who, during the excitement of boarding the *Gridley*, put the question, "How far are we from the Azores?"

"About a hundred miles from the western islands."

"Jeez, we could have made it. What about the Three and Four?"

"Commander Read made it—almost all the way. He's at Horta now."

"Good ole Putty. And the Three?"

"We don't know. They must be down. Nobody's heard from them since around noon."

5

The men aboard the Three felt gagged. During the minutes they used their port engine to power their radio they learned that Read had landed at Horta. Later they picked up news from the *Columbia* that Bellinger and his crew had been rescued. Able to hear, they were anxious to be heard, but the weak beam they were able to send out apparently plunged into the water just yards from their plane. It was frustrating; it was exasperating.

They had spent all afternoon in a kind of night. When night came by the Greenwich clock, they took heart. In the true night the destroyers would turn on their strong searchlights and thus become visible across the distances. Towers inspected his Very pistol and found it usable; on seeing searchlights he would fire the pistol and they would be rescued.

Comforted by this, they gave their thoughts to food. A few of their sandwiches were wet, but enough were dry for them to feel they would not face starvation. The candy bars were all right, and there was one emergency ration for each man. They had no drinking water.

"If we reach the point where we need water badly," Towers said, "we can drain some out of the radiators."

Around seven o'clock they ate, with no thought of rationing themselves; surely they would not be adrift so long that the lack of food would become a problem.

At eight o'clock they faced the fact that they would probably be at sea for the night. "There's no need for all of us to stay awake," Towers said. "Let's set up two-hour watches. Who feels like taking the first?"

His system so full of strychnine and caffein that he felt a little high, Richardson said, "I might as well. I couldn't sleep now unless somebody hit me with a pipe."

In their confidence, the crew smiled at Richardson. He crawled into the pilot's cockpit and tried to make himself comfortable. The others found dry spots in the hull where they could stretch out. The soft throb of the bilge pumps lulled them to sleep; the last thing Lavender could remember seeing were the strips of rags they had stuffed into the cracks in the hull. Richardson's job was relatively simple: he had only to hold the plane into the wind. It was a strange feeling, sitting there—alone, in a weird sense—looking forward but aware that he was moving backward. Staring out into the darkness, he attuned himself to the rhythm of the wind and sea, letting his body respond to each dip and sway as if he were dancing to a familiar tune. Ordinarily the monotony of it might have put him to sleep, but he knew that sleep was out of the question for him. He surveyed the hull around him; it had taken a severe beating and even now was withstanding sudden attacks that would certainly splinter the average structure to shreds. He had done a good job designing the hull; nobody could deny that. It was the hull alone that was protecting their lives. He was satisfied with himself.

McCulloch relieved Richardson at ten o'clock; Lavender took the midnight watch; Towers went topside at two in the morning, Moore at four.

Shortly before six, full awake on a heap of useless sea anchors, Richardson was roused to his feet by a loud, deep groan of wood that made him think the hull had cracked in half.

Towers said, "What was that?"

Richardson waited for a rush of water, and when it did not come he said, "Must be something topside."

They hurried to the rear cockpit, losing their footing in sharp dips of the rocking plane. First they looked at the wings; badly damaged, they were nevertheless still secure. They looked aft.

"It's the control column," Towers said.

Fresh morning winds had stirred the sea to deep waves, and the tail had apparently sunk into one of them and been severely wrenched. The control column, by which the tail was normally manipulated, had been whipped off and was thrashing against the hull, digging into the wood. The plane was beating itself to death.

X

PUTTY READ was suddenly very tired. His surprise landing at Horta had caught the Navy and the town itself off guard. The Four taxied deep into the bay before anyone realized what had happened. Then excitement burst. From the *Columbia* came the shriek of horns and whistles. Small boats came out from shore, their crews armed with flowers hastily plucked and wildly thrown at the plane. By Aldis lamp, the *Columbia* greeted: "WELCOME TO THE AZORES."

Motorboats sped out from the destroyer to escort the Four to a mooring. Read beheld the panic with weary disinterest. When the plane's engines were cut off, Read went into the hull. At this moment of triumph, his only thought was that, the engines off, the hull seemed strangely quiet.

Jim Breese came forward. "There's a motorboat standing by."

Read measured Breese with the hint of a smile. "Remember the first time you and I rode in one?"

Breese had all but forgotten the day Read had inspected the primitive training camp his rich friends had organized on Long Island early in the war. He laughed a little. "I was more scared on that trip than I was on this one."

Read gathered his papers and charts. He noticed that Rodd at his radio was jotting notes in his log, and he could tell from their soft comments above that the pilots were completing their notes. Nobody seemed eager to leave the plane.

Read said to Breese, "Have the ensign raised."

Breese located the small, triangular flag among his equipment and gave it to Smokey Rhoads to run up the slender flagpole on the wings.

At last they were ready. The motorboat from the *Columbia* had moved in close, its crew holding it fast by gripping the Four's hull and wing. Hinton and Stone climbed out of their cockpit and stood aside on the hull so that Read could be the first to disembark. As Read hoisted himself topside crewmen in the motorboat broke into applause. Perceiving this was the commander, the people in the nearby boats cheered him.

Ignoring the welcome, Read stepped out on the wing, then lowered himself into the motorboat.

The bosun saluted him. "Glad to have you aboard, sir."

"Glad to be aboard," Read said, then stepped aside to make room for his crew.

They were at the *Columbia* in a few minutes. As Read led his men up the gangway, the destroyer's crew sent up a great cheer. Read heard himself being piped aboard and smiled at the honor being given a lieutenant commander. He saluted the ship's ensign, then its captain and shook hands with the man.

"We're honored," the Captain said. Then he turned to his First Officer. "Notify Admiral Jackson at Ponta Delgada that we have guests."

They were taken to the wardroom and given hot coffee. "I wish," the Captain said, "that Navy regulations allowed for something more appropriate for such an occasion."

"The coffee will do fine," said Read.

"A hot meal is being prepared for you and your men."

"I think we'd all prefer a warm bed," Read said.

"I've thought of that, too. Quarters are being arranged for your men. You will use my room."

"That won't be necessary," Read said. "I don't want to put you out."

The Captain smiled broadly. "It will be my pleasure to be able to say that the commander of the first plane to fly across the Atlantic slept in my bed."

Read brushed aside the joke and flattery. "We haven't made it yet. There's still a long way to go. Do you have any news?"

"Not much. It looks as though the other planes are down."

"I was afraid of that. Our radios were faulty, but we managed to pick up a few messages that gave us that impression."

"The search is on," the Captain said. "The station ships in the last two hundred miles have scattered out, looking for them."

Read nodded, aware of the difficulty of locating the downed planes in so dense a fog, so severe a storm, so broad a sea.

The Captain said, "If they're afloat, we'll find them."

Read nodded again.

The hot meal was brought in.

The crew of the Four had no idea what a sensation they were causing aboard the *Columbia*. As they ate, the ship's officers popped in and out of the wardroom, some to stand and stare, others to put forth questions. To fly all the way from Trepassey to Horta was, indeed, a feat; even to be able to find the Azores, especially in a fog, was masterful navigation. But they had landed at Horta, not Ponta Delgada, and there were still almost a thousand miles separating them from the Continent. Read still did not experience any sense of conquest, nor did any of his men. Nevertheless, each man to his own degree enjoyed the attention of the *Columbia*'s officers, modestly diverting the praise and compliments with, "Wait, wait. The flight isn't over yet."

The Captain returned as the meal ended. "I've radioed Washington that you're aboard. Messages are pouring in." He handed Read a batch.

Read glanced at them. Congratulations came from Josephus Daniels, from Roosevelt, from Admiral Taylor, from scores of others. He passed them around the table.

Breese said, "Nothing from President Wilson?"

Everyone laughed. The Captain said, "He's in Paris, but I'm sure the department will notify him. Commander Read, you'll all want to be sending messages to your families, I suppose?"

"Yes, I'm sure."

"Good. There's paper on the desk. Just give the messages to one of the wardroom boys."

"Thank you."

"And, Commander, a delegation from Horta has arrived.

The Mayor wants to come aboard and welcome you officially."

Read frowned. "Now?"

"He can be here in an hour."

Read regarded his men. Their beards were heavy, their eyes were half-closed, their flight suits were smudged with grease. "We're in no condition for a reception."

"You've got time to freshen up," the Captain said. "I wish you'd do it, Commander. These people put a lot into such things."

Read's evaluating glance put the question to his men. All of them shrugged indifferently. "I suppose we'll have to."

Hinton said, "I'd like to get out of these clothes."

The Captain offered, "I can send men out to your plane for your gear."

"No souvenir hunters, please, Captain," Rodd put in. "We haven't finished with the plane yet."

Breese said, "Besides, we're passing out only one kind of souvenir."

The Captain let his brows rise knowingly. "Oh, yes. I heard about that." He joined the laughter.

There was just time for the men to send their messages home, to wash and shave and shower and change to their regular Navy aviation uniforms, then return to the wardroom to be greeted by the Mayor of Horta and his entourage. Each man was given a bouquet of flowers and a bottle of Portuguese wine, then there were speeches by a surprising number of dignitaries for so small a town. None of the Americans understood a word of the speeches, except the repeated references to "Prezeedahnt Weelzon," but they smiled as each speech ended and bowed modestly to the applause. Read made a brief response on behalf of his crew.

Read could not keep his eyes open. He was dismayed, when the speeches ended, to see that sandwiches and coffee were being carried in. Was there no end to the protocol?

He heard the Captain say to the Mayor, "American Navy regulations prohibit the consumption of alcoholic beverages aboard our ships; I regret I have nothing but coffee to offer you."

The comment was translated for the Mayor, and the translator said for him, "Ah, but you do!" And he indicated the wine given to the Four's crew.

"But regulations—" the Captain began. "Oh, the hell with regulations."

Like the others, Read surrendered his bottle of wine, but he would not drink any. One sip, he knew, would knock him out. As long as he had to endure the formalities, he decided he might as well stay awake for them.

It began to look as if the Mayor would never leave. One hour passed into another. With each passing moment, Read found it increasingly difficult to stifle his yawns. At one point he noticed that Elmer Stone had fallen asleep leaning against a wall; he moved near Stone and gave him a nudge.

The Officer of the Day came in with a message for the Captain, who glanced at it, then called across the room: "Commander Read, the *Gridley* has picked up Commander Bellinger and his men. They're all safe."

Putty Read brightened. "I'll have some of that wine now," he said.

It was after nine o'clock when the Mayor finally left, the last urgent messages from Washington had been answered and Putty Read made his way at last to the Captain's quarters. He saw that a cot had been erected in the room and he went to it.

"Oh, no," the Captain said. "Take the bunk."

"I'm too tired to argue," Read admitted.

"No argument. I've got some work to do. I'll try not to disturb you when I turn in."

"You couldn't, even if you fired cannons," Read said, and he began to undress.

He slept late—late for him. A few minutes after eight, Sunday morning, May 18, he stepped out on deck for a look at the sky. The fog had returned and he could not see the nearby shores.

The Officer of the Deck approached. "Good morning, sir."

"Good morning. How bad is this fog?"

"The entire area is socked in."

There went his plans to continue to Ponta Delgada that morning. "Is the Captain on the bridge?"

"Yes, sir."

Read went up to the bridge. "Good morning, Captain," he said as he entered.

"Good morning, Commander. Sleep well?"

"Yes, thanks."

"I'm afraid I've got bad news."

"I see it," Read said, looking out the windows. "Any word from Commander Towers?"

"No word at all."

"Strike two," said Read, quickly glum.

"I'm afraid I've got Strike Three for you," the Captain said. "Two of the British teams took off this morning from Newfoundland."

"Oh?"

"One crashed on take-off, but the other's been flying for five hours now."

"Who is it?"

"Hawker and Grieve."

Read took the news with pursed lips. "They're good men."

The Captain said nothing. Read asked, "Any reports on them?"

"No. They're not carrying radio."

Read thought about it. "Well," he said at last, "I suppose it would be 'cricket' of me to wish them good luck."

2

News of the British pilots was radio gossip that morning all over the Atlantic. Lavender picked it up and gave it to Jack Towers. He crumpled the message and let it fall into the water at his feet. "What's their weather?"

"I don't know," Lavender said.

"For their sake, I hope it's better than ours."

The continued fog and the renewed storm depressed everybody on the Three, but there was no time to brood. Massive waves crashed against the plane and threw her wildly about. The broken control column beat against the hull.

"We've got to get rid of that thing," Towers said.

"There's only one way," Moore pointed out. "Break it off."

"That's too dangerous. One man could never do it."

"I could try."

Richardson offered, "I'll go out there with you, Moore."

Towers shook his head. "No, it's too dangerous."

"Look, Jack," Richardson said, "I designed this hull and I know how much of a beating it can take. If we don't break off that beam it'll hammer right through and we'll have a hole we won't be able to patch."

Towers considered the problem. "How would you do it?"

"We can crawl out on the spars."

"Will they hold you?"

"If they're not too badly damaged."

"Won't your weight push the tail structure under?"

"Maybe. We'll get wet, but we'll be all right as long as we hang on tight."

There was nothing else to be done. "All right," Towers permitted. "But test those spars every inch."

They took tools from Moore's kit. Hoisting themselves out the rear cockpit, they wrapped their legs around the spars and, shoulder to shoulder, began to crawl. As Towers predicted, their combined weight forced the rear structure to dip toward the water. Waves hit them, and when the waves sank into the sea the structure dropped and lowered them into the water. They held their breath, they grasped at the spars, they came up coughing and blinded. But they kept crawling out.

At last they reached the place where the broken column swung on the hinge of the wires it contained. They cut at the wires, they hacked at the column itself, they twisted and bent the stubborn metal and wood. For twenty minutes they struggled, coughing, spitting, cursing, plunging into the sea. Then the severed beam dropped away. Carefully they inched their way back to the hull, relieved when they felt their feet touch its thick surface.

When they were back inside, Lavender said, "That must have been fun."

"I wouldn't recommend it," Richardson said.

They were a little safer now.

The perverse wind seemed to come from all directions, creating opposing waves that lifted the plane high between them, then broke away, leaving the plane as much as five and six feet up in the air. When the plane dropped back to the surface, she hit with a resounding wallop that made the hull tremble and let the wings sink deep into the sea. Tons of water pushed down upon the flimsy canvas strips that closed off the cockpits, fore and aft, and the hull was flooded again. Slowly the bulky hull forced the wings up out of the water, but by then the damage was done, again and again. The repeated brutality of the sea snapped the ribs of the wings, letting the fabric sag and creating deep pockets to fill with water and hold the plane deep longer on each attack. The bilge pumps were unable to remove each burst of flooding and bailing became increasingly difficult.

"It's the fabric," Moore said. "We've got to slash it so the water can get through." He reached for a knife.

"I can't let you go out there," Towers said.

"I appreciate that," Moore said, "but we ain't got much choice. Either I take the chance of being swept off out there or we all drown in here for sure. Besides—" he held up his safety belt—"I got this. It won't be any worse than going out on the spars."

Towers knew that Moore was right: there was no choice. He knew too that the job to be done was indeed Moore's, but he hated letting one of his men risk his life against such odds. But it had to be done.

Moore climbed into the pilots' cockpit next to McCulloch and from there moved up into the wings. The wind was savage, the sea a monster. Fastening his safety belt low on the struts, he worked his way, first out the starboard wing and then out the port, slashing his knife into the cloth, toughened by the water, stabbing at it from above, then leaning over to cut from beneath. Twice he rode the wings down under the surface, sputtering his anger and discomfort as the plane slowly lifted. But as he worked the reward of his efforts were quickly evident. Now, when the plane dropped from mid-air it bobbed back up to the surface with the rhythm of the sea.

When finally he returned to the hull, Towers said, "I wish I could give you a drink."

Moore said, "I wish you had one to give me."

Now they were safer than before.

They nursed the pumps. They continued to bail.

At eleven-thirty, the tip float on the left wing broke off and was immediately pulled away by the sea, beyond recovery. Now without any support to hold it up, the wing dipped into the water, forcing the entire plane to roll over dangerously. When Moore discovered what had happened, he climbed into the superstructure and hurried out to the right wing tip. Standing there, his weight was enough to level the plane.

Lavender said, "He's not going to stay out there from now on, is he?"

"No," Towers said. "We'll all have to take turns at it. That means a double watch for each of us." And that meant half as much rest for each of them.

It was like musical chairs. A man put in his two hours at the controls, then he tried to sleep for an hour, then he went out on the starboard wing for an hour, then again he tried to sleep, then either he went back to the controls or he sat at Lavender's radio and tapped out the SOS. On signal from Towers, everybody moved to his next chore—and even sleeping was a chore; the quick crests, the awesome shudder of the plane, the changing winds that spun her around kept a sleeping man too tense to rest and he got up wearier than when he lay down.

In the early afternoon the sun burned through the fog and disclosed some land clouds in the distance. McCulloch saw them first and called them to Towers's attention. Using his binoculars, Towers was quite sure he could detect the

157

mountain slopes enshrouded by the clouds. Checked against maps, the silhouette gave all appearances of being Pico. With the help of the weak sun, Towers's instruments put him forty-five miles southeast of the island.

Towers observed to Richardson, "We have enough fuel to go into Pico under our own power."

"Yes," Richardson agreed, "but can the plane take it? We're running very bad seas."

"That's what I'm considering," said Towers. "If we lose the starboard wing float against strong waves we'll roll right over."

Lavender asked, "What happens if we don't go into Pico?"

"For one thing," Towers said, "we'll have to spend at least another night at sea. With the wind we have and the speed we're making, we might reach a point near Ponta Delgada sometime tomorrow. But if the wind changes, anything can happen."

"And if we try for Pico now, the plane might break up?"

"It could," Richardson said. "At least the wings. The cross wind would be strong enough to roll us."

"I'd hate to spend another night out here," Lavender said.

"Maybe more than a night," Towers pointed out. "And we are just about out of food."

Richardson said, "Well, we know what we'd like to do. What must we do?"

"We'll have to play it safe," Towers decided. "We'll keep going."

Later in the day, Lavender reported with chagrin, "Here's a laugh. I just picked up some talk from the *Columbia*. Commander Read is socked in at Horta. We're closer now to Ponta Delgada than he is."

McCulloch took the news with a sad, sick smile. "What else is new?"

"They're still looking for us a hundred miles west of here."

"Maybe we ought to go back and help them out."

Lavender shrugged at the idea. Towers came down from the cockpit. Lavender told him, "Sounds to me like Washington wanted the Four to come out and look for us."

"In this soup?"

"That was the answer. The Four is fogbound at Horta. I was just telling Dave that the wind is pushing us closer to Ponta Delgada than the Four managed to make it by air."

"Good for us," said Towers, "but I'd change places with Putty any time."

"Me, too."

Moore came in from his second watch on the port wing. McCulloch took the safety belt from him and went out for his own second watch. He was very tired. Hours of retching on an empty stomach had debilitated him. He was still seasick, he still could not bear the thought of food, but he insisted on taking his turn on the wing. He strapped himself to a stay wire, then leaned against it. An hour later, when Towers went out to relieve him, he found McCulloch fast asleep.

Early in the night, Richardson discovered that when he held the ailerons in neutral he could steer with less effort and also acquired sufficient control to prevent the left wing from dipping. He passed the information on to Towers. Moore was again out on the wing. When Towers called him in and explained the new development, he said, "I'm glad to hear that. I've been dunked so often I'm getting waterlogged."

But Moore's trips out on the wings were not over. During

the night the wind increased to gale force, pushing the plane astern at fifteen miles an hour. Exploding waves ripped at the starboard float, loosening it until it was held in place by two thin wires only. Moore needed no explanations why it was necessary for him, as engineer, to return to the wings. Three times during the night he went out to repair the float.

Despite the terrors of the night, it offered the hope that the spotlights on destroyers could be seen more easily and that the Very pistol might attract attention. Two or three times during the night the men thought they saw a destroyer's lights, but then they realized they were seeing only the phosphorescent tips of the soaring waves.

Toward morning the wind shifted, pushing them on a more southeasterly course, away from the islands, out to sea, toward Africa. This was the risk in Towers's decision to keep going instead of trying for Pico, and it was too late for regrets. For two hours they felt themselves moving away from their destination, all of them too heartsick to discuss it.

Then, around eight, the wind changed again, now driving them northeast. With the change had come a brief clearing, and Towers took a quick bearing.

"We're heading right at Ponta Delgada," he announced.

There was a stir of hope aboard the plane.

At nine, the sun again came briefly into sight and Towers took another reading. "We should be sighting land any minute," he said.

Eager and impatient, Moore removed the canvas cover from the rear cockpit and perched himself in the seat. Although he was actually in the stern, the plane was moving backward and he was, in effect, riding the bow. It was precisely at ten-twenty-three, Greenwich, that he jumped down into the hull and yelled, "Land! Land dead astern!"

Richardson was at the controls and strained his neck for a look at the land. Towers climbed through the cockpit and out on deck for a look. Lavender joined Moore at the stern. McCulloch, trying to sleep, heard the noise, attempted to raise himself up, but he fell back and immediately began to snore.

They were still a long way from land, but they could see it and that was all that mattered. When they had soaked up enough of the sight, they went about their chores. Lavender tried once more to make radio contact with somebody, but once more he failed. Moore threw a piece of wreckage overboard, and from it Towers was able to place their speed at six knots. McCulloch got up after a while and relieved Richardson at the controls. Richardson found himself hungry and decided to try his emergency ration. It contained beans, dried eggs, dried fish, beef extract, some cornmeal. It was all tasteless, but Richardson did not mind. He took some water from a radiator and drank it as if it were wine.

They had to be careful. As they neared shore, the current increased, sending rollers across reefs and against huge rocks. To avoid being swept in by it, they held their distance from shore and aimed at the harbor on a long hypotenuse. At three o'clock, Towers estimated they would be entering the harbor in two hours. To control their speed, they put a sea anchor out, and it held. But then they hit a rain squall and a sudden shift of wind. The anchor was ripped off, sending the plane yawing badly. The port wing sank sharply, then slowly arose. They realized they were not out of danger yet.

They were still seven miles out. The fog was behind them; the sky was gray and heavily overcast, but the visibility was much improved. Lavender said, "You'd think they'd spot us by now."

McCulloch said, "I don't think they're expecting us."

Even from their distance, they could see the lighthouse, the radio station, the sugar factory, houses, trees. An hour later the farms and vineyards and roads began to take on form and color.

They were sighted at twelve minutes after four.

With their binoculars, they could see the sudden action in the harbor. Ships steamed up, bunting was raised, Aldis lamps began to flicker. The *Harding* came around and headed for the breakwater, racing out to them at top speed.

Towers called, "Moore, run up our colors!"

The Three's ensign was already in place, but it was upside down: the distress signal. Moore hurried to the wings, lowered the flag, righted it, then sent it up again.

Towers asked, "Moore, is our Aldis working?"

"I'll check," Moore said and went to the hull. He was back in a moment with the lamp and gave it to Lavender, standing topside at Towers's side. "It works."

The *Harding* was approaching fast, her Aldis flickering wildly. Lavender decoded: "They keep saying, 'It's a miracle! It's a miracle!' "

"Tell them we believe it's a miracle, too," Towers said.

The flicker conversation began. Lavender said, "They want to send out small craft for us."

"No," Towers said. "We came this far; we're going the rest of the way."

Lavender then asked, "They want to know if you want them to take us in tow."

"Tell them to stay out of the way," Towers said. "We're going in under our own power!"

The *Harding* stood by, following slowly. Lavender turned

162

his lamp on the *Melville,* in the harbor, for entrance instructions.

Four miles out, the shorebound current stiffened and the two pilots encountered increased difficulty in maneuvering the plane. "Easy, easy," Towers encouraged them. "We can swim it from here, but let's not."

At the breakwater, the right tip float broke off. The plane flopped crazily from port to starboard.

"Start the rear engine!" Towers ordered.

Moore rushed out on the starboard wing and cut the turnbuckles on the two wires to the loose float and it dropped into the water.

The engine gave the pilots a little control. Towers said, "Lavender, tell the *Harding* to have a lifeboat stand by. Then notify the *Melville* that we'll need a couple of punts to put under our wings."

Lavender flashed the messages.

Towers told the pilots, "Get some more power and head in."

Richardson turned on the two wing engines, both of them held in place only by broken supports and waterlogged braces. The wings shook violently. Moore realized that his weight on the starboard wing was causing the plane to list to the right. He made his way across the wings to the port side. Now the port wing sank below the water; the plane began to pitch. Lavender threw his Aldis lamp into the bay and dashed toward the starboard wing. In doing so, he walked directly into the roaring rear engine.

"Look out!" Towers screamed.

Lavender ducked an inch from the whirling propeller, then slid around it and out the wing. He was heavier than Moore; Moore felt himself rising high into the air as the starboard wing went down.

163

Richardson said, "Dave, can you handle the controls alone? I'd better get out on the port wing to balance Lavender."

"Go ahead," McCulloch said.

Richardson climbed onto the port wing and began to work his way out it. "Dinty," he called, "start working in."

The two men met at the middle, their combined weight leveling the plane. "I'll stay out here," Richardson said. Moore went on to the hull.

They were in the harbor now and it was a frantic bedlam. Every ship's horn blasted a greeting. Launches were everywhere, like gnats. Bands blared on the docks. Crowds lined the shores. Flags flew from the tiled roofs of every house. The arrogant launches darted in close, stirring waves. Richardson and Lavender danced back and forth on opposite wings, battling to hold the plane steady, their efforts to shout instructions to each other lost in the riot around them.

From the *Melville* came two launches pulling punts; they went to either side of the plane. The bosun of the port launch seemed uncertain of his instructions. After buzzing the plane, he roared away. But the men in the starboard launch knew their job. They swept in close, bringing the punt under the wing. The sailor in the punt grabbed at the wing. That instant, the port wing dipped. The starboard wing soared and the sailor was lifted five feet into the air and he let loose a terrified yell.

"Hang on, buddy!" Lavender called.

But the sailor could not. His fingers slipped and he dropped back into the punt, steadying it just as it was about to capsize.

The men on the port launch recognized what was expected of them. They sped into a fast turn to come back, but the turn was too fast and the punt was swamped. Men on other launches saw the problem and moved in to help, guiding

164

their boats under the wings. It was a game; as a wing lowered, dozens of arms shot up to hold it off, and the gesture was accompanied by a loud, drawn-out chorus of "Whooo-aaa!" In this way the Three lumbered down the bay to its mooring.

Standing topside, struggling to balance himself, Towers watched the merry panic and shook his head. It was all so unlike the Navy. He said, "If I didn't see this with my own eyes, I'd never believe it."

There were other things the world would have trouble believing. After a record overseas flight of 1,220 miles, the NC-3 had survived sixty hours on a wild sea, lost in a dense fog, beaten by a savage storm, and during that time she had managed to sail 205 miles—into the port that had been her destination.

As the Three limped into the harbor, a shore battery started a twenty-one-gun salute. There was something both sad and proud in the tribute, and every man felt it. To be sure, the Three was a defeated plane; she had not accomplished her mission—to fly to the Azores. But she had accomplished much more; her stubborn determination to survive was evidence of the genius of the men who had designed and built her and the courage and skill of the men who were her crew. By any standards, her arrival at Ponta Delgada was a miracle indeed and the Navy could always be proud of it.

3

Putty Read and his officers were in the *Columbia*'s wardroom when the ship's radio officer rushed in with the amazing news: "The Three has arrived at Ponta Delgada!"

Read stood up. "Arrived?"

"She sailed in."

"Good God. Is everybody all right?"

"All safe and sound."

"And the plane?"

"She's a wreck. They'll never be able to fly her again."

Dazed by the news, Read turned back to his men. "Well," he said, "I guess it's up to us."

XI

THERE WAS NO NEWS of Hawker and Grieve, but this was not unusual. Their goal was Ireland, a greater distance from Newfoundland than the Azores, and to carry enough fuel they had sacrificed their radio. They had left Newfoundland on Sunday morning, May 18, ignoring forecasts of storms along their route. Nothing was heard from them by Sunday night, long after they were expected in Ireland. However, there were many desolate expanses along the western coast of Ireland, many villages that had no telegraph or telephone connections with bigger cities. The two pilots might have landed at any of such places. Even when Monday passed with no word from them, there was concern but not despair. Still in Newfoundland, ready to take off at the first sign of improved weather, were Alcock and Brown, less impatient than Hawker and Grieve, less panicked by the departure Friday of the Americans, and much encouraged to learn that on Tuesday morning, four days after leaving Trepassey, the Americans were still in the Azores, only one of their planes was usable, and a thousand miles still separated it from Europe. There was still time to beat them.

2

Read had hoped to take off early Tuesday morning. The morning, however, was darkened by squalls all along the 150 miles to Ponta Delgada. With mountains on every islet of the route, it was decided to wait for clearing. At noon, visibility was good enough for a try. Once again destroyers lined the route, some of them ships that had been ordered into new positions after their similar duty across the Atlantic. Shortly after taking off, Read recognized the *Robinson* beneath him for the third time; she had been a station ship on the Halifax-Trepassey run, then moved out into the sea, and now she marked the way to Ponta Delgada.

At a thousand feet, visibility was excellent. Pico Island fell behind, then San Jorge, then Terceira. Stationed at every twenty-five miles, the destroyers sent up their smoke on sighting the Four, then cut it when radio acknowledgment was established. Read checked off the ships, one by one.

The flight took a little more than two hours. Looking down at the Ponta Delgada harbor, Read saw that it was so full of ships he wondered where he was expected to land. He contacted Rodd on his repaired intercom and told him to request landing instructions.

They were to come in from the sea. They made a wide

turn over the bay to give everybody a look at them, then went out to sea, banked into the wind and came in long and slow, touching down just inside the breakwater. Clusters of launches were already there, waiting to lead them in. Comfortably, almost smugly, they taxied across to the special landing that had been constructed for the NCs but which the Three had been unable to make.

When they cut their engines the sound of bands wafted to them. Read looked out at the landing and saw the horde of dignitaries watching him. In the front row, next to Admiral Jackson, was Jack Towers. Suddenly Read realized what this would mean.

He said to Smokey Rhoads, "Get some men and have the hull cleaned up. You are going to have a new commander on the next leg."

Surprised, Rhoads asked: "Who?"

"Towers."

It was Navy protocol in such situations that the squadron commander should select a new flagship; Read would lose his plane.

Read went ashore.

At Horta, Read had been an unexpected guest but the town had done its hasty best for him. Ponta Delgada was ready. He was given a twenty-one-gun salute as he stepped ashore, which embarrassed him. He was given a medal. With typical Latin effusion, the Governor kissed him, the Mayor kissed him, and he saw that a long line of lesser celebrities were prepared for the same display. He turned quickly and grabbed Towers by the hand.

Towers was genuinely pleased. "I got here first, Putty, but you made it the way we had it planned."

Pat Bellinger stepped out of the crowd, laughing. "The Lame Duck showed us up, uh, Putty?"

It was like New Year's Eve. Cameras popped and purred at Read, reporters threw questions in a dozen languages, children came forward with flowers, the Portuguese notables plunged into lengthy speeches, bands blared, crowds roared.

Read muttered to Towers, "How long does this go on?"

"God knows," Towers replied. "You should have seen what we went through yesterday—and we practically waded in."

Later in the afternoon, the Governor gave a luncheon. That night, Admiral Jackson, commander of the Azores base, was host at a formal dinner and dance. The Mayor insisted on giving an even more elaborate party the next night.

"But we won't even be here tomorrow night," Read said.

Breese danced by on this. "Don't be a party-pooper, Commander." He whirled away, his arms full of a Portuguese beauty, himself full of Portuguese wine.

Read decided he wouldn't be—at least for the evening. He accepted the wine each time a waiter approached with a fresh supply. He danced with every Portuguese woman who came near, most of them a head taller than he. It was two o'clock in the morning when the last guests departed. Read went to his room a little drunk.

The morning brought a sobering drama.

Eager for a good start on the eight-hundred-mile flight to the mainland, Read was up early. He had just put on his freshly brushed flight suit when a steward came to his room and said that Admiral Jackson wanted to see him. He finished dressing, left the Admiral's quarters and crossed the base to the Admiral's office. On entering the room, he saw Towers, dressed in his regular uniform.

"Aren't you ready?" Read asked.

"I'm not going," Towers said. His frown was heavy, his voice soft with anger.

Read looked at the Admiral. "You wanted to see me?"

170

"Yes," Jackson said. "I have instructions here—" he handed Read the message—"from Secretary Daniels that you are to remain in command of your plane for the remainder of the flight."

Read did not look at the message. "But Jack Towers is the Flight Commander."

"Nevertheless," said the Admiral, "the Secretary seems to feel that you brought your plane this far and you should take it the rest of the way."

"How did all this come about?" Read asked.

It had come about during the festive hours of the previous evening. Josephus Daniels had been out of Washington the last days before the flight and the first days of it; Roosevelt was in charge and made the decisions. Daniels returned to Washington at the hour every newspaper in America was heralding Read's successful flight in enormous headlines. A newspaper publisher himself, Daniels was sensitive to the extreme value of hero worship, sensitive to what it could do for Navy recruitment that had fallen so sharply after World War I. He would not be deprived of a hero. The decision that Read should continue the flight as commander of his plane was the Secretary's.

Roosevelt fought it, pointing out that the order was distinctly contrary to Navy tradition and regulations. Jackson fought it. So did Admiral Knapp, commander of the Navy in the European Theater. But Daniels refused to budge. Nothing the Navy had done during the entire war had captured so many front pages. The Navy had a hero—a pint-sized hero, to be sure, but that made him all the more lovable—and Daniels wanted him to go on to a hero's reception wherever he went.

"All right," Read said, "so I'm in command of the plane. But can't Jack go along as a passenger?"

"No," Jackson said. "He has orders to continue to England by ship."

Read turned to Towers. "I'm sorry, Jack. I know how long you've had your heart set on this flight; I know that without you it wouldn't have left the ground in the first place. I'm sorry."

"It's not your fault," Towers said. His tone was still harsh. "Have somebody take my flag off your plane. I was presumptuous enough this morning to have it run up." He stalked out of the room.

A half-hour later, Read was in the forward cockpit of the Four, ready to taxi into position for take-off. Again the landing pier was crowded. The Governor was there, the Mayor was there, Jackson was there, the crews of the One and Three were there, but Jack Towers was not.

On the intercom, Read gave the order: "Turn 'em over."

Quickly the four engines were turning. The Four was released from its mooring and began to move away.

Hinton called to Read, "Something's wrong with the forward engine. I can't get much life out of her."

"Breese," Read said into the intercom, "what's wrong?"

"I'll have to take a look," Breese said.

"Look."

Breese went topside. Read could hear him and the pilots on the intercom but did not catch all their words.

Hinton said, "It's the generator, Putty."

"What's wrong with it?"

"No pep. Jim says it has to be replaced."

"How long will that take?"

"Couple hours, maybe."

That meant they could not take off in time to reach the mainland before dark. It also meant that he would have to

172

go back and face Jack Towers again. He was ready to take a whipping rather than do that.

3

It proved to be an awkward, embarrassing day. Towers stayed out of sight, but his angry presence on the island was so permeating that Read found himself constantly glancing over his shoulder to see if Towers had entered the room. There was actually nothing Read could do; he had his orders. But Towers's stern reaction to them made Read feel uneasy, as if he had connived to trick Towers out of his honors. His men and members of the other crews tried to console him.

"Putty," Bellinger said, "you're in the Navy; you have to obey orders. Jack understands that."

"I suppose so," Read conceded. "I hope so."

"Forget it, Putty," Dave McCulloch said. "Jack'll get over it."

"I don't see what there is for him to get over, as far as I'm concerned," Read said. "All along, I was ready for him to take over."

"He knows that," Mitscher assured. "It's just a big disappointment for him."

Richardson said, "The way I figure it, you ought to be the man, Putty. Daniels is right. The Four didn't get this far on its own; you brought it in. You should take it the rest of the way."

"Forget it, Putty," they all advised.

It was not an easy thing to forget. When he was alone, Read comforted himself with the bitter fact that it was just tough luck for Towers that Secretary Daniels made the decision he did, but there was nothing that could be done about it. This, Read felt, was the only attitude he could take.

He did not deny to himself that there would be a certain triumph in being the first man to fly across the Atlantic Ocean, which he would be, sitting up there in the forward cockpit—provided he could ever get the Four into the air again—but he was the kind of man who could wear such a triumph quietly. It would be, after all, a triumph for every man who had anything to do with the flight, each one of them united within the anonymity of the Navy and the enormous Curtiss factories. As for Towers, maybe time would ease his disappointment. It was tough luck.

Thursday morning's take-off was canceled because the storm had kicked up again and made the bay too rough. So there was to be another day of the uncomfortable atmosphere. Friday the storm was still too bad for the Four to attempt a take-off. That afternoon, Towers and Bellinger and their crews boarded a destroyer for the voyage to England. Lou Barin said, "We'll see you in Plymouth, Putty, if you ever get out of here."

The parties were still going on, and Jim Breese said, "I don't care if we never leave."

Jack Towers approached Read. "Good luck, Putty," he said quietly.

"Thank you, Jack," Read returned.

Friday night a radio message from London disclosed that Hawker and Grieve had crashed eleven hundred miles out from Newfoundland. They were picked up by a freighter bound for Liverpool. The ship had no radio. The world had just learned what had happened to them. And there was further news, this from Newfoundland. Alcock and Brown were testing their Vickers Vimy daily and it was performing masterfully. They were only awaiting assurances of good weather across the North Atlantic to begin their flight.

Read, too, was waiting for good weather. It did not come

174

on Saturday or Sunday. On Monday there was a decrease in the wind velocity, but Read felt it wasn't sufficient to warrant a take-off; there was no sense in taking risks at this late stage. He scheduled departure for six o'clock Tuesday morning, May 27. But at six o'clock, dirt was found in the gas and the carburetor. Breese and Rhoads spent four hours cleaning it out. At ten-eighteen, the Four finally taxied out into the stream. Her load was a ton below capacity, an advantage she needed because the harbor was too short for a take-off with full load. Besides, she did not require full fuel tanks for the eight-hundred-mile journey.

The take-off was bumpy and slow; the plane passed just a few feet above the breakwater. Over open water, she rose at a cautious angle, then banked eastward.

As the Four settled down to get on course she flew directly over the first station ship. This surprised Read; his calculations put him some seven or eight degrees south of his proper course. Puzzled, he accepted the course he was on and instructed Hinton and Stone to proceed dead ahead. In half an hour, when they should have passed over the second ship, Read discovered that it was fifteen miles to the north of him. He did not sight the third ship at all.

He was baffled. There seemed small likelihood that all the destroyers were off course, but when Read tried to adjust to their locations his calculations put him far off.

He said to Rodd, "Get a radio fix on Number 4." When Rodd reported back, Read found himself thirty degrees south of the true course. A recheck seconds later put him forty-five degrees south. There was this to comfort him: as long as he kept heading east he would eventually reach Portugal or Africa—easier to find than the Azores had been. Even so, why was he so far off? Carefully he went over each of his instruments. Then he saw it: the compass had been knocked off its gimbal ring, obviously during the bumpy take-off. He adjusted it and, with relief, watched it correct his calculations. He was back on course in time to pass over Destroyer Number 7—the *Robinson*. He was glad to see it again. He relaxed.

As he approached the Portugal coast, the whitecaps below him smoothed into land swells—a welcome sight. In view of what had happened to the One and Three, the possibility of a forced landing on the high seas was never entirely removed from his mind. Seeing the long, full swells assured him that if the event became necessary it would not be difficult.

Because of the long delay in resuming the flight, Destroyer Number 10 had been pulled out of line for other duty. Thus the distance between Numbers 8 and 9 and Numbers 11 and 12 was extended to sixty-seven miles to cover the gap. It made no difference. The Four, aided by a strong tailwind, roared eastward at ninety miles an hour, as cozy as a bus. On passing Destroyer Number 13, some fifty miles off the coast, the wind dropped, cutting the plane's speed by approximately fifteen miles. With an hour left, Jim Breese shaved for the party he knew would be held for the crew at Lisbon. Read, also thinking of the party, realized he would not have time after landing to write his flight report; he did it now.

It was approximately twenty minutes after seven when Elmer Stone clicked on the intercom. "Putty, there she is."

Read went into his cockpit. There was the rocky coast of Portugal, coming at them fast. In eleven minutes they were over it.

Read waited for the waves of elation to strike him, but they did not come. His only sensation was that a job had

176

been done and he had been part of it. He picked up his log and noted that at seven-thirty-one, Greenwich time, on the evening of May 27, 1919, the NC-4, an aircraft belonging to the United States Navy, had arrived over Portugal, completing, so far as he knew, the first flight across the Atlantic Ocean. Rockaway Beach, where the flight had begun nineteen days ago, was 3,322 miles away. Actual flying time: forty-one hours and fifty-eight minutes.

It was an historic moment.

But like most such moments, moments which in a special way changed the world, the men who made them possible, who fulfilled in an instant the dreams and plans of months and years, were not fully aware of the impact of their achievement.

Jim Breese finished shaving and went to the rear cockpit with his pan of dirty water. Smokey Rhoads was sitting in the cockpit, casual eyes on the land below. Breese threw his water overboard; a few drops splashed on Rhoads; he gave Breese an annoyed frown.

"A souvenir," Breese said, "for Portugal and you."

Hinton and Stone were busy at their controls, adjusting to the air bumps coming up from the land. Rodd was at his radio, in contact with the *Rochester* and the *Shawmut* at Lisbon. Read was back in the forward cockpit, calculating his arrival time and informing Rodd of it.

At ten minutes to eight, the Lisbon sky bright purple with evening, they were at the mouth of the Tagus River. At one minute after eight they tied to their mooring astern of the *Shawmut*.

Four hundred and twenty-seven years before, almost to the day, Christopher Columbus had sailed from these very waters westward to a new world.

4

The reception at Lisbon outblared Horta and Ponta Delgada combined. Having learned from the Azores experience, the Navy vessels in the harbor quickly sent out launches to encircle the Four to keep the excited and the curious from getting too close. As soon as the plane was secured, Read and his crew were taken aboard the *Rochester* for the official reception. The twenty-one-gun salute began as Read stepped on the quarterdeck. As before, Read considered the salute a bit too much; normally it was reserved for the heads of governments or the first arrival of a foreign flag in a port. He was not the President, and the American vessels had been in port for a week.

Then came the speeches again, the medals, the citations, the handshakes and the bows, this time even more outrageously flattering than in Ponta Delgada and Horta. Finally, at eleven o'clock, it was all over.

Breese said, "Why don't we sort of hit the town for a while?"

"Aren't you too tired?" Read asked.

"Not for a little sight-seeing."

Read went with him; so did Hinton and Rodd. Their sight-seeing was restricted to nightclubs and bars. Cheering crowds followed them to every door. Owners swamped them with wines and whiskeys, buried them under hot, spicy Portuguese delicacies. Performers danced and sang at their table's edge, sometimes in their laps. They began to feel like the heroes the city acclaimed them to be.

Breese said, "I may just take out citizenship papers."

He could have had them—or anything else he wanted—for the asking. For two days the parties continued, bringing Read and his men additional honors and tributes. The *New York Times* headlined: NC-4 WINS FIRST OCEAN FLIGHT FOR

178

AMERICA." Dick Byrd, honored for his navigation instruments, declared, "The American Navy—bless her—has once more won the admiration of the world." Louis Blériot, the French pilot who in 1909 had made the first important overwater flight across the thirty-one miles of the English Channel, told reporters, "Ten years ago my flight was called extraordinary. But it was insignificant compared to the deed of the NC-4." In New York, Glenn Curtiss predicted that the flight marked the beginning of commercial transatlantic air travel—an observation many experts still considered rather reckless. And from Paris President Wilson wired Read: "WE ARE HEARTILY PROUD OF YOU. YOU HAVE WON THE DISTINCTION OF ADDING FURTHER LAURELS TO OUR COUNTRY."

The only unhappy people were the photographers and newsreel cameramen who had waited for Read for a month at Lisbon. Landing at twilight, he had arrived too late for them to take their pictures of his triumph. During the two days of parties they repeatedly asked him to make another landing at Lisbon for them to record on film. Read thought the request was a little ridiculous but finally he agreed to accommodate the newsmen. At dawn on May 30, when he was ready to resume his flight to England, he informed the photographers that he would take off at five-thirty, circle over Lisbon to give the people a final look at the plane, then make a landing for the sake of the pictures.

He took off at five-twenty-four. The sound of his plane over the city brought crowds into the streets. Breese was impressed. "These people never sleep," he said. "It's wonderful."

Then the Four moved out to sea, made a wide turn and came in for a landing close to the *Shawmut.* Launches of newsmen accompanied the plane on its run and moved in close for better pictures. One cameraman shouted, "That's fine, Commander. Now how about doing it once more—just to be on the safe side?"

"Not on your life!" Read cried. He gave his pilots orders to take off—this time for Plymouth. They took off.

Two hours later, at seven-five, the port engine began to sputter and lose power. Breese reported to Read: "Looks like a leak of some kind. We'd better sit down."

Read had feared something like this. Fortunately, the sky was clear. The sea, when they got low enough for a look at it, was running heavy swells that could push the plane ashore.

"Let's look for a river," Read said.

They flew on for another fifteen minutes, then saw a river, a small one, with a village on its southern banks. Read gave instructions to land.

They discovered that the river was the Mondego and the town was Figueira. They landed at seven-twenty-one. Concerned with their engine trouble and the task of landing, they failed to take into consideration the fact that the tide was out. Taxiing upstream, they ran onto a sand bar. By revving their engines, they managed to slide across it. After this, they were especially cautious.

The trouble, Breese found, was a leak in the radiator. Among his equipment was a mixture made expressly for such damage. He poured it into the radiator and they were ready to go in half an hour. However, the sand bars were becoming increasingly prominent and Read was reluctant to take further chances with them.

"We'll wait out the tide," he announced.

At this point, the Captain of the Port came out in a rowboat. The man spoke no English; nobody aboard the Four spoke Portuguese; an effort was made to converse in French, which the Captain of the Port spoke a little, Read spoke less and Breese faked magnificently. With the help of gestures and facial distortions, Read was able to learn that the tide would return at two in the afternoon. The Captain's invitation to lunch in town was therefore accepted.

There was another problem. Prevented by the tide from taking off until midafternoon, the Four could not possibly hope to reach England before nightfall. Still wary of any last-minute accidents that might ruin his effort, Read refused to do any night flying. By radio, he informed both the Azores and London of his forced landing at Figueira, and he requested instructions for a place where he could put up the Four safely for the night. He was ordered to proceed to El Ferrol, Spain, a two-hour flight north. This was another disappointment. Every man aboard the plane regretted it— except Jim Breese. For him it meant the chance for another night of parties.

By one-thirty-eight, the Mondego was high enough to taxi out for a take-off. With a good wind behind them, they made El Ferrol in fifteen minutes less than the anticipated time. The town was informed of the important visitors it would have for the night. By the time the plane glided into the harbor the town was well ready. So was Jim Breese.

It was unnerving, now that they were so near to their final destination at Plymouth, that the weather forecast for Saturday, May 31, was fog and rain for the entire European coast. Learning this, Read remarked that future pilots ought to be trained in patience as well as flying, adding that at this point patience was the one thing he was lacking. With an audacity unusual for him, Read decided to take off for England despite the weather.

The Four lifted into the haze at El Ferrol at six-twenty-seven and immediately plunged into fog and heavy rain. For the sake of comfort for the crew, Read altered his course repeatedly. He also noticed that Hinton and Stone occasionally took a choice of course into their own hands when the flying grew particularly rough. He let them choose their way for a while, until their constant shifts confused his own calculations.

At last Read said on the intercom, "Fellas, how about letting me decide where we're going?"

"Sorry," Hinton said.

Visibility across the broad Bay of Biscay was so bad that the plane missed four of the six destroyers stationed along the route. Flying low to catch the smooth air, Read saw that the sea was strangely calm. Always concerned with a possible forced landing, he was grateful for the calm.

Even close to the sea the visibility was bad. Read decided to foresake his course and he moved the Four inland to be sure to sight Ushant, the northwestern corner of France, an important landmark to Plymouth. Ushant was sighted, then Ras Point, then Brest. Brest was the embarkation port for eighty thousand American veterans of the war who were still waiting to go home.

"Let's give them a look at us," Read suggested.

The Four circled in the gray sky over the city, dipping its wings in salute. The commander of the American Naval forces in France sent up a radio message, inviting the crew down for a drink. Read sent his regrets, then directed his plane out over the channel. A thick haze covered most of the channel, clearing slightly as the Four approached the cliffs of England. From Plymouth came a radio message: "BRITISH SEAPLANES ALOFT TO ESCORT YOU."

Read replied: "REQUEST BRITISH CRAFT MAINTAIN SAFE DISTANCE UNTIL HAZE CLEARS SUFFICIENTLY FOR US TO SEE THEM."

He did not see them at all.

Two hours out of Ushant, he recognized the hills of Plymouth and ascended to fifteen hundred feet for a survey of the harbor. He saw the *Aroostock,* an old friend from Trepassey. He saw, too, the great crowds on the docks, spilling over into the network of streets. At that moment, the Royal Air Force seaplanes came out of the channel fog and assembled in formation above him. Below, from the guns of a British warship, impatient puffs of smoke bellowed: the twenty-one-gun salute. On orders from Read, the Four moved out toward sea, then banked and headed in. Read looked at his watch. It was twenty-six minutes after one.

The job was finished.

A correspondent of the *New York Times* reported:

Flying straight for the *Aroostock,* the great plane turned west, flying along the whole length of the front, turning again around the western end of Drake's Island and again at the Citadel, and taxied into the sheltered Cattewater, where she anchored to a buoy in the very mouth of the River Plym and within a stone's throw of the Mayflower stone on the Barbican.

As I swept up to her she looked like some huge, gray porpoise, covered with a staging of yellow, upon which the small figures of human heads could be seen moving jerkily, while the British planes which had escorted her danced many lazy figures of sheer joy-riding and of the aviators' brotherly interest in the great victory achieved over the atmosphere and the mechanical difficulties.

The streets were filled with cheering crowds all the way to the Grand Hotel on the Hoe, where, within sight of the greens on which modern Englishmen play Drake's great and historic game, the American aviators were welcomed to England.

XII

IN 1954, Jim Breese, then a successful inventor and prosperous Arizona industrialist, had the occasion to go to Europe on business and he decided to fly. A stewardess aboard the flight, as part of her professional graciousness, strolled the aisle, chatting with the passengers. She asked Breese, "Is this your first overseas flight?"

"No," said Breese. "I've flown across once before."

"When was that?" the young woman asked.

"Thirty-five years ago."

Her eyes widened, impressed, but as she went on her way she became puzzled. Thirty-five years ago? What airline was flying the Atlantic then? She entered the control cabin

184

and remarked to one of the pilots, "There's a man back there who said he flew across the Atlantic for the first time thirty-five years ago. Is that possible?"

The pilot thought about it. "It's possible. He might have been on the NC-4. Ask him to come up here."

It was the first time in years that Breese had encountered anyone who knew of the flight, and it was sad that this should be so. For some reason, perhaps because it took place too soon after a war that people were trying to forget or on the eve of the Roaring Twenties in which they succeeded in forgetting, the flight that was undoubtedly the most important in aviation since the first one at Kitty Hawk disappeared from the annals of America's air history. The hero whom Josephus Daniels wanted enjoyed a brilliant but extremely brief public career.

All England was Putty Read's during the week he spent there. The Prince of Wales—later the Duke of Windsor—went up in a plane over London and put on a stunt show for Read's entertainment. The King of England awarded him the Royal Air Force Cross. The House of Commons asked him to lunch. President Wilson, at a summit conference in Paris, summoned Read and presented him with the U.S. Distinguished Flying Medal and introduced him to others of the Big Four—Clemenceau, Lloyd George and Orlando. Then all Paris threw itself at Read's feet with startling Gallic abandon. From Paris he went to Brest to accept the drink from the Navy commander there and tributes from the city. After Paris, Jim Breese found Brest too calm, so he went back to Paris. On June 27, when the crews of the three NCs boarded an ocean liner at Brest, Breese was still at a Paris hotel. Jim Towers had no alternative but to send him a telegram charging him with being absent from duty without leave and promising reprimand

185

the next time they faced each other. The reprimand was Breese's only punishment.

At home, Read was subjected to more receptions, more parades, more dinners, more speeches, more tributes. The NC-4, dismantled in England and shipped back to New York, was reassembled and displayed in Central Park. Hungry souvenir hunters walked off with more than a quarter of the plane's structure. Refitted, it was flown by Read and his crew down the East Coast and up the Mississippi on the recruitment stunt Josephus Daniels had in mind.

On a return visit to New York, the Four was put on display at the Battery. Once again souvenir hunters ravaged her, this time so badly that she sank. The Navy raised her, outfitted her again, then moved her away from the piers for her own protection. At this time, a New England Congressman happened to be in New York and, in a show of influence, offered to arrange for two of his lady friends to board the plane. The Navy refused. Long afterward, when Congress discussed presenting the plane's crew with a special gold medal, the New Englander was the only man to vote against it. The medal was finally struck in 1929 and presented to the crew by President Herbert Hoover.

Despite the fact that the flight and the men who made it topped front-page headlines daily for a month, the historic event faded quickly from the public mind. The fact that America had won the air race across the Atlantic was given its cheers, then forgotten. The fact remained unaltered even though Alcock and Brown surpassed it in a way when, on June 14, they flew nonstop from Newfoundland to Ireland, a distance of almost two thousand miles. To them went the fifty-thousand-dollar prize money which the American Navy fliers could not accept. Oddly enough, the prize was paid out twice. During the week Hawker and Grieve were missing, the *Daily Mail* gave each of their families $25,000 as a tribute to the courage of the lost pilots, and after they were found they were allowed to keep the money. But the honor for the first transatlantic flight was America's; it was pocketed, patted, then put out of mind.

For those who treasured great events, however, men like the pilot of Breese's plane in 1954, the flight of the NC-4 would be remembered with special pride. Charles E. Lindbergh took the occasion to refer to it after his solo flight to Paris in 1927. He said:

"When I stop to think about it logically, I know that I had a better chance of reaching Europe in the *Spirit of St. Louis* than the NC boats had of reaching the Azores. I had a more reliable type of engine, improved instruments and a continent instead of an island for a target. It was skill, determination and a hard-working, loyal crew that carried Read through to the completion of the first transatlantic flight."

The flight won many firsts. It had the finest air-radio equipment of its time, all of it invented by Lavender. The radio compass, the air-to-ground, air-to-air and intercom radio systems were all produced by him to meet exigencies of the pioneer flight. It was also the first time the bubble sextant had been used, plus the wind-and-drift indicator, both these vital navigation instruments developed by Dick Byrd. The hull designed by Richardson became the prototype for future seaplanes; the hulls on the PBYs of World War II were Richardson's hulls. The hulls of the enormous seaplanes that made the first transoceanic commercial flights were based on Richardson's work. The flight of the Four was the longest sustained flight on record; the six hours the One spent being buffeted by the rough seas before rescue of the crew was a record in survival, which was quickly surpassed by the three-day experience of the Three. In addition, the flight established the Great Circle air route to Europe, which is still used, and it gave America a world lead in aviation that it never relinquished. Undoubtedly even more impressive was the fact that despite the hardships of the flight, despite the fact that two of the planes were forced down and one of them was damaged beyond salvage, not one man was lost, not one man even seriously injured. This fact, too, was evidence of skill and genius.

Within the Navy, the flight had far-reaching effects. A month after it, Navy officials who recognized its importance announced: "Aircraft have become an essential arm of the Fleet. A Naval Air Service must be established, capable of accompanying and operating with the Fleet in all waters of the globe."

In 1920, Congress created the Navy's Bureau of Aeronautics to replace what before had been merely the Aviation Section. The first Bureau consisted only of a Navy captain and two secretaries, but it went quickly to work. That same year it began work with Carl Norden on the Norden bombsight and with Elmer Sperry on his automatic pilot. Four years later, in 1924, the Navy acquired its first aircraft carrier, the *Langley,* from which planes could take off for landings ashore. In 1928, a pilot landed on a carrier, the *Saratoga,* for the first time; he was Marc Mitscher.

There were, however, some Navy leaders who did not realize the importance of aviation to the Fleet, and since, in many cases, these were the older men who filled the higher offices, they ineluctably stood in the way of proper recognition of the men who gave the Navy its first dramatic wings. None of the men associated with the flight of the NCs achieved a rank higher than captain for fifteen years,

188

a peculiar oversight in view of their contributions to Navy aviation. It was during Roosevelt's first term as President that he sent for Jack Towers and asked why he had not as yet become an admiral. Towers said he had no explanation for it. Roosevelt then created a new Naval office, assigned Towers to it and gave him his first star. Towers's chagrin over having to surrender command of the NC flight to Read at the Azores lingered for years. Even his recognition that Read had no part in the decision did not soothe his disappointment, and it was said among men who knew them both that the friendship between Towers and Read was never again the same. Added to this was the pain of watching the world so quickly forget the great air conquest Towers had worked hard to effect, and the wound deepened when fast aviation progress enabled Lindbergh to make his solo flight to Paris in 1927, thereby overshadowing the triumph of the NCs even further.

The obscurity that enshrouded the flight so soon after it made history also sent its crews in all different directions, some of them to meet again as the years passed. Richardson was in and out of the Navy several times, retiring and being recalled for special duty. He was retired again, with the rank of captain, when he died in 1960. Lou Barin went into student-pilot training. One day a student taxiing across a field plowed into the plane in which Barin was awaiting take-off instructions. He was killed. Marc Mitscher, Barin's co-pilot on the NC-1, happened to be at the base that day and saw his old friend die. Rodd, the Four's radioman, died in a crash. Glenn Curtiss continued to be a leader in new ideas for aircraft design, but his appeal as a public figure was overshadowed by his numerous legal suits, particularly with the popular Wright brothers, over the infringements of patents. As a result, Curtiss never received the esteem he deserved for his contributions to aviation progress. Despite their legal battles, the Curtiss and Wright companies merged in 1929, shortly before Curtiss's death.

During World War II, Jack Towers served as deputy commander of the Navy and Army forces in the Pacific. He eventually became a full admiral and was head of the Bureau of Aeronautics before his death in 1955. Mitscher commanded the *Hornet*, which participated in most of the important Pacific landings, and it was from the decks of his flagship that the Doolittle raid took off for Tokyo. After the war, as a full admiral, he was commander in chief of the Atlantic Fleet. He turned down the position of Navy Chief of Staff shortly before his death in 1947. Bellinger acted as wartime commander of the air wing of the Atlantic Fleet. For a while during the war Read was chief of staff of the Atlantic wing, then was assigned to train submarine fighters at Norfolk. He became a rear admiral upon his retirement.

Like its crew, the NC-4 soon suffered obscurity. The fast progress of aviation after World War I quickly made the plane obsolete, even as a show piece. Taken to Washington a few months after its recruitment tour, the plane became a white elephant. On some unknown day, it was dismantled, its parts scattered to Navy warehouses across the country. Not until after World War II was there any curiosity about it, and the curiosity came mostly from Paul Garber, curator of the Air Museum of the Smithsonian Institution. He inquired about the plane, but nobody knew where it was. In fact, few Navy men in the Pentagon had ever heard of it. By painstaking detective work, Garber was able to locate the pieces—in Virginia, in Pennsylvania, in New York. After great effort he was able to convince the authorities to ship the dissected plane to him, and he had it assembled and put on display in a building adjacent to the museum. With similar energy, he likewise convinced Congress that America's many magnificent contributions deserved more specific recognition. Due to his efforts, funds were appropriated in 1959 for the construction of a National Air Museum, to be erected on the mall near the Institution. According to plans, the principal display in the main hall would be the NC-4, which Garber described as "the most overlooked aircraft in history."

By the spring of 1961, there were few men left of those who had given the NC-4 and her sister ships their moments of greatness. Lavender, who had been an attorney on the Manhattan Project, was in Washington. Pat Bellinger was in retirement across the river in Virginia. Smokey Rhoads was living quietly in Los Angeles. And there was Putty Read.

At seventy-four, he was still alert, spry, reserved, shy, dividing his time between his apartment in Washington, his Virginia Beach house and his home at Coral Gables. With the same quick, acute mind that had made him one of the outstanding navigators in aviation, he could recall clearly every moment of the event that gave him a distinct place of honor among men for all times.

He was the first man to fly across the Atlantic Ocean.

He had changed the world.

Index

194

Lawrence, Charles, 13, 14, 15, 16, 17, 19
Liberty engines, 18, 20, 29, 34, 47, 74
Lindbergh, Charles August, 40, 187, 189
Lisbon, 177–79
Lloyd George, David, 185
Locke Body Company, 32, 33
Lodge, Charles, 14, 18, 19–20
London *Daily Mail* prize, 3, 10, 43, 45, 71–72, 97, 186–87

McCulloch, Dave
  flight to Washington, 35, 36–38
  pilot on NC-3, 47, 48, 50, 56, 65, 66, 79, 80, 82, 83, 98, 99, 114, 115–16, 117, 120, 124, 131, 145, 156, 157, 159, 161, 162, 163–64, 173, 174, 185
McDermot, the, 60, 62–63, 64, 66
McKean, J. S., 43
McNab's Island, 67
Melville, the, 163, 164–65
Mitscher, Marc (pilot on NC-1), 47–48, 51, 58–59, 60, 81, 99, 102, 104, 111, 112, 116, 122, 125, 126, 127, 128, 129–30, 136–37, 138–40, 143, 173, 174, 185, 188, 189
  World War II, 190
Mondego River, 180, 181
Monomoy Point, 59, 60
Montauk Point, 56
Moore, L. R., "Dinty" (machinist on NC-3), 78, 79–80, 103–04, 105–06, 124, 130–31, 145, 154–55, 156–57, 159–61, 162, 163, 164, 174, 185
Morgan, Bill, 49
Moulton, Harry D., 40

"Nancies," 6
Nantucket, 60
Naval National Guard, Brooklyn, 13
NCs, 1–6, 28, 29, 30, 31, 33, 34, 35–38, 40–41, 42–43, 45, 46, 47–48, 49, 50, 51–52, 177, 187, 188, 189 (*see also individual listings*)
altitudes, 6, 54, 57, 58, 59, 63, 64, 81, 82, 88, 93, 108, 111, 112, 113, 114, 115, 116, 117, 121, 122, 123, 124, 125, 126, 133, 168, 182
anchors, 130, 145, 161
British competitors, 71–72, 94, 95–96, 97, 99, 105, 153–54, 167–68
bumps, 57, 58, 59, 116, 120, 177
course, 59, 60, 62–63, 109, 114, 118, 121–22, 123, 124, 126, 127, 132, 133, 134, 135, 158, 160, 175–76, 182, 187
fatigue, 120–21
flagship, *see* NC-3
food, 3, 119, 137, 138, 144, 158, 161
fuel, 81, 95, 96, 124, 133, 167, 175
generator, 131
hull, 2, 65, 68, 83, 127, 130, 137, 145, 146, 154, 156, 187
instruments, 46–47, 49, 54, 59, 98, 99, 112, 114, 116, 117, 121, 124, 125, 158, 175–76, 187
intercom, 57, 58, 61, 75, 122–23, 168, 187
landings, 67, 80–83, 84, 89, 90, 92, 127, 135–36, 168–69, 177, 181, 183; forced landings, 63–64, 68, 90, 112, 127, 180
mail, 105
name, origin of, 6
press, 1, 2–5, 72, 97, 170, 178–80, 183–84, 186
propellers, 73, 75, 76, 77, 79–80, 96
pumps, 128, 129, 130, 136, 144–145, 156, 157
radio bearing, 124, 127
radio comunication, 56, 57, 58,

Parker, Captain, 36
Patrol ships (*see also* Destroyers *and under individual name listings*), 10, 60, 62–63, 64, 66, 72, 73, 75, 78, 80–81, 82, 83, 87, 89, 90, 91, 93, 94, 96, 97–98, 99–101, 102, 105, 109–10, 111, 112–13, 114, 116–17, 118, 121, 122, 123, 125, 132, 133, 135, 136, 142–43, 147, 148–50, 152, 153, 158, 162, 163, 164, 165–66, 168, 175, 176, 177, 178, 179, 182, 183, 188
Pensacola, 11
Philip, the, 126, 132
Pico, 132, 158, 160, 168
Plymouth, 180, 181, 182–83
Ponta Delgada, 98, 134, 135, 149, 150, 153, 158, 160, 161, 162–65, 168–74, 178
Pontoons, 31
Porte, J. Cyril, 11, 12, 30, 72
Portugal, 168, 170, 172, 175, 176, 177–79
Prince of Wales, 185
Promotions, 188–89, 190

R-34, 49
Racquet Squadron, 12–20, 61
Ras Point, 182
Raynham, Fred, 49
Read, A. C., 16, 17–19, 20, 48–49, 191
    commander of NC-4, 45–55, 56, 57–58, 59–60, 61–64, 65, 66, 67–69, 70, 72–73, 74–75, 76, 77, 83, 84, 85–87, 88, 89–90, 91–93, 95, 96–97, 99, 100–01, 102, 103, 104, 105, 106, 107, 108–09, 110, 114, 115, 116, 119–20, 122, 125–26, 129, 133–36, 143, 147–53, 158, 159, 165–66, 168–77, 178, 180–82, 183, 185, 186, 189
Read, Mrs., 48, 65

Rhoads, Eugene S. (machinist of NC-4), 53–54, 57–58, 62, 64, 68, 69, 70, 75, 83–84, 86, 89, 90, 91, 99, 101, 110–111, 123, 148, 169, 175, 177, 185, 186, 191
Rhodes, Braxton (engineer on NC-3), 105–06
Richardson, Holden C., "Dick," 24–25, 28, 29–30, 31, 33–34, 35–36, 37, 38, 187, 189
    pilot of NC-3, 47, 48, 50, 56, 65–66, 73, 78, 79, 82, 83, 96, 98, 99, 103, 114, 115, 116–17, 120–21, 124, 126–27, 131–32, 144, 145, 154–55, 158, 159, 161, 163–64, 173, 174, 185
Robinson, George, 35–38
Robinson, the, 168, 176
Rochester, the, 177, 178
Rockaway Navy Base, 1–6, 34, 35, 40, 43, 45, 47, 49, 50, 51, 52–55, 64, 74, 84, 86, 177
Rodd, Herbert C. (radioman on NC-4), 56, 58, 59, 62, 63, 64, 67, 68–69, 70, 75, 86, 88–89, 92–93, 104, 110, 115, 122–23, 126, 148, 151, 168, 175, 177, 178, 185, 186, 189
Rodgers, John, 11
Rolls-Royce, 27, 28, 29
Roosevelt, Franklin Delano, 14, 15, 16, 20, 23, 41, 42, 49, 50, 57, 64–65, 74, 76, 88, 150, 171, 189
Royal Air Force, 182, 183
Royal Air Force Cross, 185
Royal Navy, 183
Rutan, Joe, 14, 15, 16, 17, 18

Sadenwater, Harry (radioman on NC-1), 56, 58, 66, 104, 113, 115, 124–25, 129, 136, 137, 138–39, 140, 142, 174, 185
Saint John's, 71, 72, 81, 97, 99
Saint Pierre, 91

About the Authors

HY STEIRMAN was born in Montreal, Canada, and was educated at McGill and Columbia Universities. During World War II he served in the Royal Canadian Air Force as a flight lieutenant. Mr. Steirman has been an editor at Street & Smith and Hillman Periodicals, and he has written for *True, Argosy, Coronet,* and other national periodicals. He is now vice-president and editor of Paperback Library, Inc.

GLENN D. KITTLER, author, editor, and world traveler, was born in Chicago. He was an editor on the *South Pacific Daily News* during World War II and reported for newspapers in Illinois, Virginia, and North Carolina after the war. Mr. Kittler is the author of eleven books and his work has appeared in *The Saturday Evening Post,* the *Reader's Digest,* and other national magazines. He writes a weekly syndicated column and is roving editor for *Guideposts.*